EDUCATION
and
SCIENCE

KETER BOOKS

This book is compiled from material originally published
in the *Encyclopaedia Judaica*

Cat. No. 25072

ISBN 0 7065 1331 2

Printed by Keterpress Enterprises, Jerusalem

CONTENTS

CONTRIBUTORS

Dr. Moshe Avidor; Former Ambassador and Director General of the Israel Academy of Sciences and Humanities, Jerusalem

Dr. Chanoch Rinott; Senior Teacher and Director of the Center for Jewish Education in the Diaspora, the Hebrew University of Jerusalem

Bezalel Shachar, M.A.; Lecturer in Adult Education, the Hebrew University of Jerusalem

Aharon Yadlin, B.A.; Member of the Knesset; Secretary-General of the Israel Labor Party, Kibbutz Ḥazerim

Marcia Gitlin, B.A.; Journalist, Jerusalem

Prof. Norman Bentwich (deceased); Emeritus Professor of International Relations, the Hebrew University of Jerusalem

Lt. General (Res.) Yaakov Dori (deceased); first Chief of Staff, Israel Defense Forces, and President of the Technion, Haifa

Meyer Wolf Weisgal; Chancellor of the Weizmann Institute of Science, Reḥovot

David Atzmon, M. Jur.; Ministry for Foreign Affairs, Jerusalem

Miriam Balaban, B.A.; Editor and publisher, Jerusalem

Part One:

EDUCATION IN ISRAEL

1 EDUCATION IN EREZ ISRAEL

Pre-Mandatory Era (1880–1918). Education in the small *yishuv*,[1] numbering about 25,000 in 1880, largely resembled the traditional types prevailing in Jewish communities elsewhere. The Jews of East European origin maintained the traditional *ḥeder, talmud torah,* and *yeshivah,* where Yiddish was the language of instruction; the Sephardi and Oriental Jews sent their boys to the *kutab*,[2] where they studied in Ladino or Arabic. A little Hebrew was taught, mostly as the sacred tongue. Few girls, if any, attended the schools. Several attempts to establish modern schools were made in the second half of the 19th century. In 1856 the Laemmel School was founded in Jerusalem by a wealthy Austrian–Jewish family to provide secular and religious education in German; its "modernity" aroused much opposition. In 1864 the Evelina de Rothschild School for girls was opened in Jerusalem; in the 1870s it was transferred to the ownership of the Anglo-Jewish Association, changing its medium of instruction from French to English. In 1870 the Alliance Israélite Universelle established the first agricultural school in the country—Mikveh Israel.

THE PHILANTHROPIC SCHOOL SYSTEMS. Toward the end of the 19th century and at the beginning of the 20th, a number of schools were established by European Jewish philanthropic organizations, while the Anglo-Jewish Association continued to expand the Evelina de Rothschild School. The Alliance Israélite Universelle established schools using French as the medium of instruc-

---

[1] i.e., the Jewish "settlement" or community in Erez Israel.
[2] Sephardi equivalent of *ḥeder.*

3

tion in Jerusalem, Jaffa, Tiberias, and Safed and later in Haifa. The German-Jewish Hilfsverein der Deutschen Juden (known as Ezra), formed in 1901, soon outdid the Alliance: by 1913 it was maintaining 27 schools in the country, ranging from a kindergarten to a teachers' training college. German was the chief language of instruction, but Hebrew was being taught by competent teachers. The Jewish Colonization Association (ICA)[3] maintained some of the schools in the villages, and early in the 20th century the Hovevei Zion[4] in Russia helped to support some educational institutions.

HEBREW EDUCATION. The First Aliyah,[5] in the 1880s, brought to the newly established villages, as well as to Jerusalem and Jaffa, Jews who believed in a national revival and wanted Hebrew to be the language of instruction in the schools they established for their children. In the early 1880s, Eliezer Ben-Yehuda[6] started teaching Hebrew as a modern language in an Alliance school in Jerusalem. Other teachers bravely ventured into new territory by teaching arithmetic, geography, and other subjects in Hebrew, undertaking the difficult task of devising terminologies and preparing textbooks as they went along. It was in the new villages that Hebrew teaching and Hebrew speech in daily life spread more quickly. Young teachers fired by Ben-Yehuda's example taught Hebrew as a living tongue in the village schools, and general subjects were also taught in Hebrew. The establishment of Hebrew kindergartens—the first in Rishon le-Zion in 1898—contributed greatly to the spread of spoken Hebrew at home and in the street.

[3] ICA, philanthropic association to assist Jews in depressed economic circumstances or countries of persecution to emigrate and settle elsewhere in productive employment.

[4] "Lovers of Zion," members of Hibbat Zion, a movement first established in Russia (1882) which eventually merged with the World Zionist Organization.

[5] There were several waves of Zionist immigration to Erez Israel, each of which is known as an Aliyah ("ascent").

[6] Eliezer Ben-Yehuda (1858–1922), Hebrew journalist and compiler of a famous Hebrew dictionary, was the pioneer of the modern Hebrew revival.

The Laemmel School in Jerusalem, founded in 1856. Courtesy Central Zionist Archives, Jerusalem.

The Second Aliyah, which started in 1904, gave a further impetus to the growth and extension of Hebrew education. In 1906 a group of young teachers, aided by the Ḥovevei Zion in Russia, established in Jaffa the first Hebrew secondary school, the Gymnasia Herzlia which moved to Tel Aviv in 1909. This daring venture roused enthusiasm in the country and among Zionists abroad, especially in Russia, hundreds of whom sent their children to study in it. In 1908 the Hebrew Secondary School was founded in Jerusalem, and in 1913 the Reali Secondary School was opened in Haifa. In 1906 the Bezalel School of Arts and Crafts, the first essay in secondary vocational education, was established in Jerusalem.

THE TEACHERS' ASSOCIATION. There was a growing need for some national body to give guidance to individual teachers and schools in methodology and terminology, syllabuses and curricula. Toward the end of the 19th century, in the absence of an organized Jewish community in the Land of Israel, the Hebrew teachers made several attempts to organize themselves. In 1903 Menahem Ussishkin,[7] on a mission to the country on behalf of Ḥovevei Zion, convened a conference of teachers at Zikhron Ya'akov, which laid the foundation for the Hebrew Teachers' Association. This association, especially in its early years, did a great deal to strengthen Hebrew education, drawing up syllabuses, publishing textbooks and educational material for teachers, improving the status of teachers, and organizing refresher courses and in-service training. It exercised many functions that were later assumed by the organized community and, after 1948, by Israel's Ministry of Education and Culture.

The ever increasing importance of Hebrew in education, as well as the strength of the Teachers' Association, became apparent in the autumn of 1913, during what was known as the "Language Conflict." The question arose as to what language should be used in the technical institute *(Technikum)* due to be opened in Haifa. The institution, sponsored by the Hilfsverein, was financed by contributions from its own funds, Zionist sources, and American Jewish donors. The Hilfsverein insisted that German be used, whereupon the Zionist members of the institute, headed by Aḥad Ha-Am[8], resigned and a storm of protest swept the *yishuv.* The teachers rose up in arms: most of those in the Hilfsverein schools resigned, and their association, with the assistance of Zionist bodies, opened 11 parallel Hebrew schools, creating the nucleus of a national Hebrew school system headed by a board of education. The "Language Conflict" marked the beginning of the end of the Hilfsverein's educational work in the Land of Israel; when the country was conquered by the British in 1917–18, their schools, being enemy (German) property, were handed over by the military authorities to the Zionist Organization.

[7] Menaḥem Mendel Ussishkin (1863–1941), a leader of the Ḥovevei Zion and one of Theodor Herzl's earliest supporters, was from 1923 until his death chairman of the Jewish National Fund.

[8] Aḥad Ha-Am ("One of the People;" pen-name of Asher Ginzberg, 1856–1927), essayist and philosopher, called for a type of Zionism that would make Erez Israel the "national spiritual center" of the Jewish people.

Under British Rule (1918–1948). During the 30 years of British rule in Palestine, a Jewish school system was created and developed, mainly by the efforts of the Jewish community itself. Throughout the period there were two parallel school systems, Arab and Jewish. The Arab school system was taken over by the British authorities from the Turkish rulers, substituting Arabic for Turkish as the medium of instruction, and was maintained mainly by the government. These schools were attended largely by Muslim children, Christian Arab children receiving their education mostly in denominational or missionary schools. The Jewish schools were by and large the responsibility of the Jewish community, although some of them were private or were supported by Jewish bodies abroad. The Mandatory government's Department of Education, which fully controlled the Arab school system, maintained only nominal supervision over the Jewish schools. There was no law of compulsory education during the Mandatory period, and only about half the Arab children attended school for four years or more. The Jewish community, however, succeeded in providing almost universal schooling for its children. The Jewish school population grew almost tenfold during the Mandatory period and totaled nearly 100,000 in 1948.

From the Jewish Agency to the Va'ad Leummi. The Jewish national school system, born in 1914 after the "Language Conflict," was administered by a Jewish Board of Education, which controlled some 40 kindergartens and schools by 1918 and over 100 in 1920. From the beginning of the 1920s the Zionist Executive (from 1929 the Jewish Agency) maintained and administered these schools. At first it contributed some 90% of the cost and aimed at bringing all the Jewish schools under its management. Before long, however, financial difficulties forced the Zionist Executive to curtail its educational budget, which was constantly reduced and by 1932 was only 42% of the system's expenditure.

Gradually, the financial responsibility for the maintenance of kindergartens passed into the hands of local bodies; secondary schools mostly fended for themselves by introducing high tuition fees, and the vocational schools secured assistance either locally (for example from the Histadrut[9]) or from Jewish bodies outside the country, such as ORT[10] and WIZO[11]. The Zionist Executive's financial responsibility was limited mainly to the elementary schools and the teachers' training colleges. Not infrequently, financial difficulties caused delays in the payment of salaries to teachers, which brought about teachers' strikes, sometimes for several weeks.

The view gained ground, in Zionist circles as well as in the *yishuv* itself, that the financial and educational responsibility for the school system ought to be transferred to the organized Jewish community in Palestine. In the later 1920s, the Jewish population gradually assumed greater financial responsibility for the education of its children, both by paying tuition fees and by self-taxation. It was therefore accepted as a logical and natural development that control of Jewish education in the Land of Israel was formally transferred, in the autumn of 1932, from the Jewish Agency to the Va'ad Le'ummi, the Jewish National Council. The Jewish Agency continued to be represented on the governing body of the educational system and to contribute annually to its budget, although its share in the late 1930s was less than 8% of the total.

ADMINISTRATION OF THE JEWISH NATIONAL SCHOOL SYSTEM. In the years 1932–48, the national school network continued to expand under the control of the Va'ad Le'ummi, despite the general weakness of its authority and the poverty

[9] The Histadrut (founded in 1920) is Israel's major federation of labor.
[10] ORT, a name formed from the Russian initials of the Society for the Encouragement of Handicraft, was founded in Russia (1880) to promote vocational and agricultural training. Now an international body, ORT runs many schools and courses for Israel's youth.
[11] WIZO (the Women's International Zionist Organization), a counterpart to America's Hadassah, was founded in London (1920) and promotes child care, vocational training and club activities for adolescents, as well as family welfare schemes.

of the financial resources it could devote to education. Another factor contributing to the lack of unity in the educational system was the growing assumption of responsibility for the control of education by the Jewish local authorities and especially by the political parties and bodies, through the "educational trends" (see below). Four bodies were involved in the administration of the Jewish national system of education in this period: the Va'ad Le'ummi, which exercised supreme authority over major policy and approval of budgets; the executive committee of the school system, which took administrative and financial decisions—it had six members: three, including the director of Jewish education, appointed by the Va'ad Le'ummi, and one representative each of the Jewish Agency, the Tel Aviv municipality, and the central administration of the Jewish settlements; the Education Committee (Va'ad ha-Ḥinnukh), appointed biennially by the Va'ad Le'ummi, consisting of 13 members representing various political and educational trends (including three teachers and one person nominated by the Hebrew University), which dealt with educational matters and functioned only in an advisory capacity; and the Department of Education, consisting of the director of education and the chief inspectors of the three "educational trends," which was the executive body administering the current work of the school system.

THE SCHOOL SYSTEM: STRUCTURE AND CONTENT. The Jewish school system in the Land of Israel in 1918–48 included kindergartens, elementary and secondary schools, and teacher-training colleges. The kindergartens, for the three-to-five age group, were highly popular and well developed. Most of them were maintained by local authorities and women's voluntary organizations; others were run privately by their teachers. They fulfilled an important social function by enabling mothers to go out to work as well as the educational function of preparing the children for school. Moreover, they played a significant part in welding together the heterogeneous Jewish population, with its divergencies of language, culture, and modes of life. The toddlers introduced the Hebrew language into their homes, as well as often unfamiliar habits of hygiene and the taste for new foods. In its own special way the kindergarten became an important instrument of adult education in the broadest sense, particularly among the mothers. Elementary schools, consisting of eight grades, were attended between the ages of 6 and 14. They were open six days a week, the first four grades studying four hours daily, and the higher grades five to six hours, in one session. Schools in the kibbutzim had both morning and afternoon sessions. From the very beginning, Jewish educators had to cope with the difficult task of coordinating and integrating Hebrew and general subjects in the curriculum. About one-third of teaching time was devoted to Hebrew subjects, which included on the average four to five periods of Bible a week in all grades. The rest of the time was devoted to general subjects, including arithmetic, history, geography, science, art, singing, physical education, handicrafts, gardening, and, in the four upper classes, English. In the religious schools more periods were devoted to Hebrew subjects.

Most of the Jewish secondary schools followed the Central European pattern. They comprised 12 years of study, the first eight of which paralleled the elementary school. As they charged considerable tuition fees, attendance was restricted, and many pupils joined them only in the ninth year of study, after completing eight grades in the elementary schools. Although financially independent of the Va'ad Le'ummi, the secondary schools accepted its educational supervision and presented all their graduates for final examinations conducted by its Department of Education. These examinations were responsible for the development of a more or less uniform curriculum for Jewish secondary schools throughout the country. The kibbutzim and moshavim, however, maintained their own secondary school system which did not prepare its pupils for final examinations or diplomas. These secondary schools also combined Jewish and general studies. In the two upper classes, pupils could choose between programs emphasizing humanistic or scientific studies. In addition to English, they had to take a second foreign language: Arabic or French.

The teacher-training colleges were usually based on five or six years' study, the first three or four paralleling the upper grades of the secondary schools and the last two offering mainly pedagogical training. One section trained kindergarten teachers and the other elementary school teachers. Secondary school teachers were usually university trained.

The Va'ad Le'ummi controlled, financially or education-ally, two-thirds of the Jewish schools in the country. The rest were very varied: eight Alliance Israélite Universelle schools with about 3,000 pupils, where Hebrew and French were the media of instruction; the Evelina de Rothschild School in Jerusalem, with Hebrew and English as languages of instruction; a number of vocational schools maintained by voluntary bodies; *talmud torah* institutions and yeshivot of the Orthodox religious type, some using Yiddish; and the nucleus of a network of Orthodox elementary schools controlled by Agudat Israel[12] In addition, both the Hebrew University in Jerusalem and the Haifa Technion opened their gates for regular studies in 1925 as autono-mous institutions.

THE EDUCATIONAL "TRENDS." When the Va'ad Le'ummi assumed control of the national school system in 1932 it was already divided into three "trends": General, Mizrachi,[13] and Labor. Between 1918 and 1920 the national school network was unified, but it included some schools, comprising about 20% of all the pupils, which were specifically religious in character. In 1920 the London Zionist Conference decided to recognize two categories of Jewish national schools in Palestine: schools of a general

[12] A world organization of ultra-Orthodox Jews, founded 1912.
[13] Mizrachi, a worldwide movement of religious Zionists (founded 1901) which operates within the overall Zionist framework. In conjunc-tion with its labor and kibbutz wing, Ha-Po'el Ha-Mizrachi, it forms the National Religious Party (NRP or Mafdal).

character, designated as belonging to the General Trend; and religious schools, which were included in the Mizrachi Trend, named after and affiliated to the religious Zionist movement.

The General Trend tried to combine national and general progressive values in its education. While maintaining a positive attitude toward Jewish religious tradition, it left religious observance to the individual pupils, in accordance with the desires of their parents. The schools of the Mizrachi Trend, while providing a general education, laid emphasis on religion, and their principals, inspectors, and teachers were observant Jews. In the early 1920s the Jewish labor settlements, both kibbutzim and moshavim, began to organize their own schools, which combined general education with labor ideology and new approaches to educational methods. Such schools were soon established by labor circles in towns as well, and in 1926 the Zionist Organization accorded them a recognized status as the Labor Trend, affiliated to the Histadrut, which by 1938 was included in the administrative network of the Va'ad Le'ummi education system. Each of the three trends, while forming part of the national system, enjoyed considerable autonomy in drawing up the curriculum and appointing teachers and inspectors. Each was led by a school council of ten to twelve members (including parents, teachers, and inspectors) headed by a chief inspector selected by the trend, who represented it in the Department of Education. The chief functions of the council were to protect the interests of the trend, nominate inspectors, hear their reports, and appoint representatives on various educational bodies. Toward the end of the Mandatory period, 53% of the pupils belonged to the General Trend, 24% to the Mizrachi, and 23% to the Labor Trend.

The Orthodox schools of Agudat Israel, as well as the yeshivot and other non-Mizrachi religious institutions, including those of the old *yishuv*, remained outside the national system and formed de facto a separate trend, in which secular subjects were eliminated or drastically reduced. Toward 1948 about half of them were maintained and controlled by Agudat Israel and the other half by the old *yishuv* and others. Together their pupils numbered about half as many as those in the Mizrachi schools.

While the variety of curricula and the freedom of each trend to try new experiments was all to the good, the splitting up of the national system into three separate groups, to a large extent separately administered, was not always beneficial to education, particularly since not only the Mizrachi and Labor trends were backed by political bodies but the General Zionist parties also assumed some sort of responsibility for the General trend, and rivalry among the trends was sometimes instigated and abetted by the sponsoring parties. This situation became anomalous in the early years of statehood, when political parties supported "their" trends in an effort to attract more pupils from children of newly arrived immigrants who knew little or nothing about the differences between them, believing that by placing a child in one of the schools of its "trend" it would thereby also gain its parents' votes at election time.

RELATIONS WITH THE MANDATORY GOVERNMENT. Up to 1922, the British administration gave no financial assistance to the Jewish schools in the country, which were considered "private schools." At first the Zionist Executive was satisfied with this situation, for many Jewish leaders and educators preferred to have an autonomous educational system, without government interference. The British administration, with limited resources at its disposal, was content to deal with the education of the Arab children; even then it could not meet more than about one-fifth of their needs. As the enrollment in Jewish schools grew and the Zionist Executive began to find it difficult to meet all its financial obligations to its education system, it requested the support of the British administration, which made small annual grants to the Jewish schools in the years 1922–26. The Jewish authorities asked for a grant based on the number of Jewish pupils at school and for an allocation per pupil equal to the cost of an Arab pupil in the government

13

schools. The government objected, as this would have entailed allocating to the Jewish schools nearly half the educational budget, whereas the Arabs constituted about five-sixths of the population. In 1927 the government decided to allocate the money in proportion to the size of the Arab and Jewish populations. In 1933, it adopted a new formula, dividing the grant in proportion to the total numbers of Jewish and Arab children between the ages of five and fifteen in the country, as officially estimated. Thus, while government grants for education increased almost every year, they averaged only about 10% of the Jewish educational budget.

The Mandatory government's Education Ordinance of 1933, regularizing the administration of schools, recognized the Va'ad Le'ummi schools, heretofore technically "private," as "public." The ordinance referred to the "Hebrew Public System" as paralled to the "Arab Public System," which was under direct government control. When the government increased its grant to Jewish education in 1927, it insisted on formal approval of its budget, improvements in its administration, and the participation of a government representative in an advisory capacity on the executive committee of the Jewish national system. The government Department of Education, which had a small Jewish inspectorate for Jewish schools, interfered little in their affairs, although from time to time it offered suggestions for administrative and structural reforms. In 1945, at its initiative, a government commission was sent out from England to examine the administrative machinery of the Va'ad Le'ummi education system and its report, published in 1946, proposed far-reaching reforms. This report was still under discussion when the Mandate ended.

BUDGET AND FINANCE. With the reduction in the contribution of the Jewish Agency to the maintenance of education, the *yishuv* itself had to assume ever greater financial responsibilities for the school system. While in the early 1920s it provided only 10–20% of the funds required, its share rose by 1933 to about 80%. Table 1 shows the sources of income of the Jewish school system in the 1940s. A striking feature was the large percentage of school costs paid by parents. Only the kibbutzim and the moshavim

Table 1. Income of Jewish School System, 1942/43 & 1944/45

	1942/43 PL	Approximate %	1944/45 PL	Approximate %
Palestine government	92,741	11.5	127,082	8.5
Jewish Agency	46,500	5.7	116,760	7.9
Va'ad Le'ummi	19,286	2.3	41,721	2.8
Jewish local authorities and communities	326,173	40.0	556,000	37.3
School fees	305,000	37.0	584,000	39.2
Miscellaneous	30,300	3.5	64,000	4.3
Total	820,000	100.0	1,489,563	100.0

provided free education. To these must be added the Tel Aviv community, which found it possible to abolish elementary school fees by defraying the cost of schooling out of the municipal budget. Only a small registration fee was demanded of parents and this, too, was remitted in whole.

ON THE EVE OF THE ESTABLISHMENT OF THE STATE OF ISRAEL. The Jewish national education system under British rule had many weaknesses: it controlled only 65% of the Jewish schools; it was never accorded full legal recognition; it invariably had to contend with financial difficulties; and the trend system enfeebled its administrative unity. Nevertheless, it not only grew tenfold during the period from 1918 to 1948 but also developed the attributes of a state system of education. The national system embraced kindergartens, elementary and secondary schools, trade and agricultural post-secondary institutions, and teacher-training colleges. It included special schools for handicapped children, school luncheons, health services, school clubs, and extracurricular activities. A great deal of attention was paid to curricula and methods of teaching. Rules were laid down for teachers' terms of service, and the Teachers' Association grew into a powerful professional body. In addition to the network of schools maintained or supported by the Va'ad Le'ummi, there were numerous private and semi-private schools, a system of evening schools for working youth maintained by the Histadrut, and a large number of evening courses for adults in which newcomers learned Hebrew and adults could pursue further knowledge in the sciences, humanities, and foreign languages. The State of Israel thus inherited a network of schools which could be easily converted into a state school system.

2 EDUCATION IN THE STATE OF ISRAEL

Legislation. The organized framework of Jewish education which had been developed in the main by the organized Jewish community in Palestine paved the way for the Compulsory Education Law passed by the Knesset in 1949. This law marked the beginning of a period of continuous expansion due, on the one hand, to the influx of new immigrants and, on the other, to the inclusion in postprimary and university education of an ever-increasing proportion of students. There was also a marked increase in the number of Arab pupils. By 1973, the school population had reached a total of almost 920,000, contrasted with the figure of 140,000 in 1949. The school population reflected the changes in the composition of the country's population produced by the successive waves of immigrants with their different cultural and social backgrounds. The place and manner in which the newcomers were housed and absorbed were important factors in the development of the educational system. In many cases immigrants founded their own towns or villages, in others they settled in existing population centers, notably in the suburbs. Thus schools were opened in which pupils were entirely or predominantly newcomers, sometimes from many different countries, sometimes with a common background. The school thus played an important role in the spread of the Hebrew language and culture, as well as in the process of welding and integrating the newcomers and the population as a whole into a single nation.

The Ministry of Education and Culture was established

Children at play in a kindergarten, 1951. Courtesy Jewish Agency Photo Service, Jerusalem.

in April 1949, its first minister being Zalman Shazar.[1] The transition from the educational system of the Mandatory period to state education in Israel took some time. The main problems the new ministry had to tackle were the "trends" (see above), compulsory education, educational administration, and the organization of Arab education. The Compulsory Education Law of 1949 made education obligatory and free for: (1) children aged 5—one year of kindergarten; (2) children aged 6-14—eight years of primary school; (3) youth aged 14-17 who had not completed their primary education. The law reflects some of the special conditions of education in Israel. A year of kindergarten was necessary to insure that all children entering primary school were sufficiently acquainted with Hebrew, which in many cases is not the language of the

[1] Shnéur Zalman Shazar (Rubashov: 1890–), author, journalist, and Labor Zionist leader who became third President of the State of Israel (1963-73).

home. At the other end of the scale, special provision had to be made for boys and girls above primary school age whose primary education was incomplete, either because of the absence of compulsory education in Mandate times or because of the inadequacy of the education they had received in their countries of origin.

Responsibility for the implementation of the law was divided between the government (educational programs, inspection, training, appointment, and payment of teachers) and the local authorities (buildings and maintenance). The local authorities are permitted by the law to demand from parents a payment for "special services," such as books and other educational prerequisites, school meals, insurance, and supplementary education, graded in accordance with the parents' means.

The State Education Law of 1953, the second basic act of educational legislation—introduced by Shazar's successor, Ben-Zion Dinur[2]—had as its main purpose the transfer of administrative and pedagogic control of education from the "trends" to the state. However, the new law gave parents the choice between state education and state religious education. Within the general framework of the Ministry of Education and Culture, state religious education enjoys pedagogic autonomy, which safeguards the religious element in school life, in the syllabus, and in the appointment of teachers and inspectors. The former Agudat Israel "trend" opted out of the state educational system and maintains an educational network of its own, under the category of "nonofficial recognized schools."

The law formulates principles and directives, giving overall authority to the minister. It stipulates that primary education is to be based on the values of Jewish culture and the achievements of science; on love of the homeland and

---

[2] Ben Zion Dinur (1884–1973), professor of Jewish History at the Hebrew University of Jerusalem, was also a Mapai (Labor Party) member of the Knesset (1949–57).

devotion to the state and the Jewish people; on training in agricultural work and handicraft; on fulfillment of pioneering principles; and on the aspiration to "a society built on freedom, equality, tolerance, mutual assistance, and love of mankind."

The almost total implementation of the Compulsory Education Law in the Jewish population, and to an appreciable extent in the Arab population too, has led to the continuous expansion of postprimary education. Even before primary education became compulsory, 85% of those who completed the eighth primary grade continued their education in a postprimary school, while 60% of Jewish children finished a postprimary school. This process was accelerated by the introduction of graded tuition fees in postprimary education. As a result, in 1971/72, 56.3% of all postprimary scholars enjoyed total exemption from tuition fees and over 20% partial exemption. This development pointed to the need for the prolongation of free compulsory education, which was started in 1970.

The Structure of the Educational System. The educational system has five stages: nursery school for children aged 3–4; compulsory kindergarten for children 5 years old; compulsory primary education for pupils aged 6–13 (8 years); postprimary education for students aged 14–17 (4 years); and higher education. In 1963 Zalman Aranne[3], the minister of education and culture, appointed the Prawer Commission, named after its chairman, to study the question of prolonging compulsory education. This involved reappraisal of the structure of the system as a whole. The commission reported in 1965, recommending the prolongation of compulsory education, in the first instance, for an extra year, and the reorganization of the school system. Instead of eight years of primary, and four years of secondary schooling, the commission proposed a six-year primary school followed by a three-year intermediate

[3] Zalman Aranne (1889–1970), a Histadrut and Mapai leader, was twice minister of education (1955–60, 1963–69).

An elementary school class in kibbutz Ha-Ogen, 1964. Courtesy Government Press Office, Tel Aviv.

school (the 7th, 8th, and 9th years) and three years of secondary education proper. The basis would thus be $6 + 3 + 3$, instead of $8 + 4$, in a comprehensive school, with its own administration, syllabus, and staff. The commission admitted the possibility, where local circumstances warranted it, of a six-year postprimary school (i.e., $6 + 6$), provided that the first three years formed a separate autonomous unit, both pedagogically and administratively.

In 1966, the government announced its intention to extend compulsory education by two years and implement the main recommendations of the Prawer Commission. In view of the opposition of the Teachers' Association, a special parliamentary commission was appointed in May of the same year to examine the structure of the educational system. In March 1968, it reported in favor of the Prawer Commission's proposals, and the government started preparations for carrying them out. In 1972/73 there were 21

127 schools, with 38,828 pupils, organized on the new basis.

School Population. During the school year 1972/73 the educational system in all its five stages had a total population of some 920,000 (including 133,000 Arabs), distributed as shown in Table 2. Of the Jewish children, 68.5% studied in State primary, 70.2% in State intermediate, and 73.3% in State postprimary schools; 25.1% in State religious primary, 29.2% in State religious intermediate and 22.7% in State religious postprimary schools; while 6.4% studied in Independent (Agudat Israel) primary, 0.6% in Independent intermediate, and 4% in Independent postprimary schools.

The Ministry of Education and Culture. The main functions of the ministry are to maintain and develop the educational system, to ensure suitable educational standards, to train and guide teachers, to inspect educational establishments, to develop educational programs and curricula, to improve teaching conditions, and to organize and encourage educational cultural activities for adults. While, owing to the special circumstances in Israel, the ministry's work is in the main centralized, it cooperates with local authorities and other public bodies in Israel and Jewish organizations in the Diaspora, and maintains contact with international educational organizations. In addition to the minister, there have been for several years two deputy ministers.

The administration is headed by the director general and a number of assistant directors general. The pedagogic direction of state religious education is by law in the hands of the director of the Division of Religious Education. Certain powers and consultative functions are entrusted to public bodies like the Public Council for Secondary Education and the Council for Religious State Education. The ministry is in close contact with the Knesset Commission for Education and Culture. In the ministry itself there are two standing committees, one for primary, the other for postprimary education, dealing with all questions of program, teacher training, and inspection. The inspectors and instructors work under their guidance. At the head office in Jerusalem there are six district offices charged with pedagogic inspection and ensuring the implementation of regulations and directives.

The budget of the Ministry of Education and Culture for 1971/72 (for details see Table 4) was IL650,000,000—6.5% of the national ordinary budget, second only to the

Table 2. School Population by Type of Institution (1948/49, 1959/60, and 1972/73)

Type of Institution	1948/49	1959/60	1972/73
GRAND TOTAL	140,817	580,202	918,702
Educational system	134,887	555,226	821,202
Academic institutions	1,635	11,300	50,000
Other institutions	585	13,676	47,500
HEBREW EDUCATION	129,688	533,948	785,355
Educational system	127,470	508,972	687,855
Kindergartens	25,406	75,699	121,135
Primary schools	91,133	357,644	368,879
Schools for handicapped children	—	7,213	12,886
Schools for working youth	—	10,197	4,074
Intermediate schools	—	—	38,828
Post-primary schools	10,218[1]	55,142	135,579
Secondary schools	6,411	24,565	54,492
Secondary evening schools	—	3,762	411
Continuation classes	1,048	7,065	7,036
Vocational schools	2,002	10,167	63,778
Agricultural schools	—	5,016	6,683
Other post-primary schools	—	1,490	—
Preparatory classes to teachers' training colleges	757	3,077	3,179
Teachers' training colleges	713	3,077	6,474
Academic institutions	1,635	11,300	50,000
Other institutions	583	13,676	47,500

Table 2 (cont.)

Type of Institution	1948/49	1959/60	1969/70
ARAB EDUCATION	11,129	46,254	133,347
Educational system	7,417	36,982	133,347
Kindergartens	637	4,956	14,921
Primary schools	6,766	30,799	101,153
Schools for handicapped children	—	—	117
Schools for working youth	—	77	222
Intermediate schools	—	—	5,221
Post-primary schools	14	1,029	11,222
Secondary schools	14	968	9,381
Vocational schools	—	—	1,272
Agricultural schools	—	23	569
Other post-primary schools	—	38	
Teachers' training colleges	—	121	491

[1] Estimate.

allocation for defense—as well as IL44,000,000 for school buildings. Additional funds for school buildings come from the National Lottery, the Ministry of Housing, the Israel Education Fund of the United Jewish Appeal, and local authorities, the development budget for 1971/72 totaling over IL190,000,000. The budget of the Ministry of Education and Culture, together with certain allocations that appear in the budgets of other ministries, covered 57% of the total national expenditure on education in 1967/68. The remainder came from local authorities, fees, public organizations in Israel and abroad, and private sources. Since 1967 subventions for higher education have come mainly through the Jewish Agency. The ministry has continuously increased its contribution to education—primary and, more particularly, postprimary—in development areas. While it covers 60% of the tuition fees in postprimary schools throughout the country, it covers 100% in the development areas. In the late 1960s it wholly maintained more than 200 primary schools and more than 370 kindergartens in new immigrant areas and granted generous

Table 3. Schools in the Educational System, by Type of School (1948/49, 1959/60, 1972/73)[1]

GRAND TOTAL	1,342	4,159	(6,118)
HEBREW EDUCATION	1,286	3,892	(5,780)
Kindergartens	709	2,008	3,775
Primary education			
Primary schools	467	1,149	1,206
Schools for handicapped children	—	82	162
Schools for working youth	—	270	115
Intermediate schools	—	—	127
Post-primary schools	98	353[2]	(490)
One-type schools	—	—	357
Multi-type schools	—	—	133
Secondary schools	39	87	204
Secondary evening schools	—	26	6
Continuation classes	33	95	63
Vocational schools	26	60	297
Agricultural schools	—	30	29
Preparatory classes to teachers' training colleges	—	—	11
Teachers' training colleges	12	30	37
ARAB EDUCATION[2]	56	267	(338)
Kindergartens	10	120	241
Primary education			
Primary schools	45	138	284
Schools for handicapped children	—	—	4
Schools for working youth	—	1	7
Intermediate schools	—	—	28
Post-primary schools	1	7	(78)
Secondary schools	1	5	59
Vocational schools	—	—	21
Agricultural schools	—	1	2
Teachers' training colleges	—	1	2

[1] In 1969/70, changes were made in the mode of counting of the institutions, and the data have been reconstructed accordingly. Institutions with more than one type of education are counted separately for each type of education.

[2] Including biennial schools and part-time evening schools.

Table 4. State Budget for Education in 1971/72 (excluding development)

	IL millions	Percentages
Primary education	444.1	67.8
School meals	12.7	1.9
Post-primary education	67.3	10.3
Supplementary education	7.2	1.8
Gadna	4.9	0.7
Teacher training	27.8	4.3
Culture and adult education	28.3	4.3
Educational television	5.7	.9
Information services	4.7	.7
Agricultural education	14.9	2.3
Higher education	4.8	.7
Administration and sundries	27.9	4.3
Total	650.3	100.0

subsidies to local authorities and various organizations for the development of vocational and agricultural education. In 1962, Education Minister Abba Eban[4] initiated the Education Fund of the United Jewish Appeal, which obtains money from the United States for the development of educational and cultural institutions in new immigrant settlements, including the erection and equipment of comprehensive schools.

Jewish Education. Jewish education is based on the following principles:

(1) The imparting of Jewish knowledge and values and the deepening of identification with the Jewish people in the Diaspora. State religious schools and those of Agudat Israel provide religious education, each according to its lights, while the other state schools represent a variegated spectrum, ranging from those in which Jewish tradition plays an important part to those from which the religious

---

[4] Abba Eban (1915–), Israel diplomat, was Minister of Education (1960–63), deputy Prime Minister (1963–66), and Foreign Minister from 1966.

element is almost wholly absent. In the course of the years there has been an increasing awareness that polarization between the religious and secular outlooks weakens the links with Jewry and Jewish tradition. There has been a growing desire to preserve the knowledge of tradition and its sources, of Jewish prayers, laws, and customs, as part of the Jewish national outlook. This led the ministry to introduce measures to foster "Jewish consciousness" as an essential part of the curriculum and the educational aim of all schools.

(2) Education for citizenship based on a knowledge and love of country and readiness to give pioneer service wherever its vital interests demand it—in settlement on the land, industry, science, and so forth. The schools of the kibbutz and moshav in particular inculcate the values of their movements and emphasize personal realization of their ideals. Civic education is an important factor in the integration of the various elements of the population. Schools, except for some religious ones, are coeducational.

(3) Education in universal human values and international fraternity; a thorough general education; the strengthening of the attachment to the world as a whole and to the peoples of the Middle East in particular. The curriculum reflects an effort to strike a balance between Jewish and general education, and aims at the development of the child's personality and capacities, and preparation for participation in the country's social, economic, and cultural life.

Israel education has had a great influence on Jewish education in other countries. Israel teachers take up posts in Jewish schools abroad, while many teachers from the Diaspora come to educational establishments in Israel, notably the Hebrew University in Jerusalem and the Jewish Agency's Greenberg and Gold Institutes, for refresher or intensive courses, to become better acquainted with life in Israel, and to exchange views with local educators. Israel participates in the work of international educational organizations, notably UNESCO, and maintains contact with institutions and educators in many countries. There is extensive cooperation with developing countries, based on Israel's own experience in promoting the education of the underprivileged.

NURSERY EDUCATION. In 1972/73 the number of pupils in state nursery schools and kindergartens was 121,135, of whom about half were five-year-olds receiving free, compulsory education and the rest 3- or 4-year-olds, in addition to children in kindergartens not subject to ministry inspection. Children aged 3–4 in newcomers' settlements or in city suburbs classified as requiring special attention received free nursery or kindergarten education. At this stage children are also introduced to the red-letter days in the Jewish calendar and the basic facts about the country's landscape and climate. In 1958 the "intensive approach" was adopted in kindergartens with the object of fostering the intellectual growth of the children in preparation for primary school by developing their ability to grasp everyday concepts in mathematics, nature, and science. The Montessori method is used experimentally in the education of disadvantaged children. Special efforts are made to encourage the active cooperation of parents.

PRIMARY EDUCATION. In 1972/73 primary education embraced some 385,000 pupils in 1,483 schools, including 162 special schools and 115 schools for working youth. In 1954, the ministry issued to all primary schools a detailed syllabus containing a graded program in Hebrew language and literature, Bible, history, geography, natural sciences, mathematics, English, French or Arabic, crafts, agriculture, domestic science, music, art, and physical training. Pride of place in the school curriculum goes to the study of the Bible, and interest is enlivened by visits to historical sites dating from biblical times. In the religious schools more attention is devoted to Talmud, religious laws, and prayers, sometimes at the expense of the sciences. The class teacher ("form master") devotes an hour a week to topics of the day and discussions on subjects of cultural or social interest.

English and, to a lesser extent, French and Arabic are the

foreign languages taught in the sixth to eighth grades. There is, however, a tendency to advance the study of the foreign languages and begin in the fifth grade. Domestic science and nutrition are linked to the school meals service which provides children with a daily hot meal in school, 80% of them receiving it free of charge or for a reduced payment.

The school program is assisted by special school radio broadcasts—16 hours a week (including four in Arabic) with special broadcasts for teachers. In addition, on a separate network established by the Rothschild Foundation, educational television broadcasts are conducted in English, mathematics, biology, and natural sciences. Each lesson is broadcast two or four times a week throughout the year. Uniformity of program has helped the cultural and social integration and consolidation of the younger generation as a unifying factor among the diversified traditions and backgrounds of their parents. However, with the passage of time, there has been an increasing tendency to allow more flexibility and differentiation in curricula and educational methods.

In the years of mass immigration immediately after the foundation of the State of Israel, the main effort was naturally directed to the provision of buildings, essential equipment, and teachers. Many of the latter were, through force of circumstances, unqualified. Dissatisfaction with educational achievement soon made it necessary to devote more attention to the special requirements of children coming from socially and culturally underdeveloped countries. Initial efforts were directed to the kindergarten—to prepare children for primary education, and to the upper grades of primary school—to prepare pupils, especially in Hebrew, English, and mathematics, for postprimary education. The problems in the postprimary school were both educational and economic. In 1954, steps were taken to meet the economic problem, at least in part, by the introduction of graded tuition fees and an increase in the number of grants awarded to the children of newcomers by the ministry and the Jewish Agency.

The improvement among children of Asian-African origin has been twice what it was among those of European-American origin. But the number of the teenagers at school is still only 44.2% among those of Asian-African origin as compared with 77.5% among those of European-American origin. The gap is greater in the domain of general (academic) schooling which is the prelude to higher education—respectively, 16% compared with 47%.

In 1965, after a series of experiments, the ministry established the Center for Schools Requiring Reinforcement, a category which in 1969/70 included 392 primary schools with 117,000 pupils in 4,354 classes—30% of the total primary school population. Of these 40% were in state schools and 60% in state religious schools. The center developed the following programs:

(1) An extended school day four times a week. (2) An extended school year—11 months instead of 10. These enabled pupils to do their homework under supervision and direction and to engage in extracurricular activities and sports in congenial conditions. (3) Inter-class grouping in three main subjects—Hebrew, English, and mathematics. Pupils in the sixth, seventh, and eighth grades were grouped in these subjects at three levels—advanced, average, below average. (4) Extra instruction in the three Rs in grades 1–5, including remedial teaching and group work with the object of helping backward pupils to reach the standard of the class. (5) Teacher guidance with a view to improving teaching methods, particularly in grades 1–5. (6) Enrichment courses in special centers for gifted children in the sixth, seventh, and eighth grades. These centers, each catering to a number of schools, provide educational and cultural activities. (7) Teacher-counselors, specially trained to advise and assist teachers, especially in the seventh and eighth grades, and to advise parents and children on the pupil's future after completing primary school. (8) Syllabus revision, guidance in the preparation of textbooks, improvement of school equipment, instructional aids, libraries, school newspapers, etc.

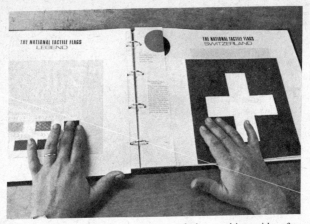

A Braille geography textbook, one of the teaching aids for the blind produced in Israel. Courtesy Government Press Office, Tel Aviv.

A countrywide scholastic test (Heb. *seker*) was held annually in the eighth grade to determine which pupils were best suited for academic postprimary education. The *seker* also provided a criterion for the award of graded tuition fees. To encourage disadvantaged pupils, the standard required from them was somewhat lower than that demanded of normal pupils. On the basis of the *seker* and the school mark, about 40% of the pupils were accepted into academic postprimary schools. With the adoption of the school reform proposed by the Prawer Commission, the abolition of the *seker* and drastic changes in the matriculation examination *(bagrut)* were among the measures scheduled for the 1972/73 school year.

In 1972/73, special education was provided for nearly 13,000 handicapped children of primary school age in 162 special schools, as well as those dealt with in special classes in regular schools. Over half of the former were of low intelligence; about 2,000 suffered from emotional disturbance and neglect, and were given special treatment and

31

education, as well as vocational training; a further group of 2,000 were chronic invalids, deaf or hard of hearing, blind, etc., and were educated mainly in residential schools run jointly by the ministries of Welfare, Health, and Education and Culture. The Ministry of Education and Culture and the local authorities jointly set up 32 psychological stations for diagnosis and classification of handicapped children, but only those in the large cities were fully equipped and provided full service, and many schools, especially in small towns and villages, received no psychological service.

POSTPRIMARY EDUCATION. Postprimary education, which is not compulsory, is not provided by the state. In pre-state days, the postprimary schools were private, but since 1949 the local authorities have increasingly provided postprimary education and their schools now form the large majority. At the same time, increased participation by the ministry in postprimary education, coupled with its responsibility for public examinations, particularly at matriculation, has increased its control over postprimary schools. The ministry's prerogatives include the determination of programs and the approval of appointments of teachers and inspectors. In addition to a Standing Committee for Postprimary Education, the ministry has a directorate for postprimary education, which is charged with (1) planning and financing construction; organizing schools and granting recognition; (2) the determination of graded tuition fees and the award of scholarships; (3) the establishment of comprehensive schools, residential schools for gifted students, and special enrichment programs in day schools.

The main objectives of the ministry's policy for the development of postprimary education are: (1) the provision of postprimary education for all, up to the age of 17; (2) in view of the general predilection for academic schooling, to induce more parents and children to choose vocational postprimary education; (3) to provide a more flexible and varied program in all forms of postprimary education and to establish comprehensive schools to increase the postprimary school capacity and prevent

Chemistry lesson in a Jerusalem school. Photo David Harris, Jerusalem.

dropout; (4) to provide special reinforcement programs for the disadvantaged in the regular schools, and enrichment programs for the more gifted, in residential schools, when necessary. The distribution of pupils between the different types of postprimary education is given in Table 2. About 40% of the pupils were in academic secondary schools, 5% in continuation classes, 50% in vocational schools, 5% in agricultural schools, and 2% in preparatory classes for teachers' seminaries. The numbers receiving academic secondary education had increased since 1959/60 by 80%, vocational education by 530% and agricultural education by 33%.

In postprimary academic education there are the following curricula: humanities (including yeshivot), social sciences, mathematics, biology, oriental studies (particularly Arabic and oriental culture), pedagogics (mainly in the preparatory classes of teachers' training colleges). Choice of curriculum is generally made at the end of the tenth grade by parents and students in consultation with teachers. At the end of the 12th (final) grade, the students are examined in five subjects for the matriculation certificate, which is required for admission to university. External students, most of whom study in night schools, take a special matriculation examination, and are required to take six subjects. In recent years the ministry has inaugurated a certificate of completion of studies for students who pass the matriculation in two or three subjects. They can obtain the matriculation certificate if they subsequently pass in the rest of the subjects. The institution of this certificate has reduced dropout after the tenth grade. In 1971/72, 11,859 matriculation certificates were awarded. Some postprimary schools have introduced two- or three-year courses in practical nursing, youth leadership, secretarial work, and so forth.

The policy in the educational system of Israel is for the State, as such, to give preference to pupils of Asian-African origin over those of European-American origin. As things are now, there is a gap between the achievement levels of pupils from different strata of the population. The policy of special care for particular strata of the population is designed to prevent the widening of the gap and to move in the direction of its closure.

The problem of dropout is particularly acute for pupils from the oriental communities, many of whom are hampered by economic and other difficulties. A follow-up of the results of the 1956 *seker* showed that of the pupils coming from Africa and Asia who passed at the A level, only 60% went on to postprimary studies, and of these only 27% completed the course. In an attempt to reduce dropout, especially from academic schools, a series of measures has been adopted: the extended school day; supervised prepa-

High school class at Yemin Orde, a religious youth village near Haifa. Courtesy Jewish Agency Photo Service, Jerusalem.

ration of homework in school, with special aids; extra lessons and courses in the summer vacation; and additional guidance by experienced teachers. About a thousand gifted students—some newly arrived, some whose countries of origin were in Asia or Africa—who, because of local conditions, were unable to make progress commensurate with their talents, were transferred to residential schools, ten in number, in various parts of the country. Such students continue to receive special attention in higher education. Special preparatory courses held at the Hebrew University and the Technion have resulted in a noticeable decrease in dropout. Table 5 shows the percentages of various origins at significant stages of the school system and in different types of schools.

Vocational postprimary education was still in its infancy in 1949, but the basis laid by the working youth organization Ha'No'ar ha-Oved, Hadassah[5], the Technion, and other

[5] Hadassah, the Women's Zionist Organization of America, was founded in 1912 by Henrietta Szold; it has made a vast contribution to health, educational, and social welfare projects in Israel.

Table 5. Pupils in Jewish Schools by Grade, Type of School, and Origin (percentages)

Grade and type of school	Origin [1]			
	Europe-America	Asia-Africa	Israel	Total
Primary schools				
1961/62 [2]	43.0	49.8	7.2	100.0
1966/67 [2]	31.6	59.3	9.1	100.0
1969/70 [2] (total)	26.9	61.2	11.9	100.0
Grade II	21.6	63.0	15.4	100.0
Grade VIII (total)	33.8	57.4	8.8	100.0
VIII in intermediate schools	22.4	73.2	4.4	100.0
Post-primary schools [3]				
1961/62	67.4	26.2	6.4	100.0
1966/67	56.7	35.6	7.7	100.0
1970/71 (total)	45.0	43.6	11.4	100.0
Grade IX	34.4	54.7	10.9	100.0
Grade XII	54.0	34.8	11.2	100.0
Secondary schools	56.0	32.0	12.0	100.0
Preparatory classes for teachers' training colleges	52.2	30.1	17.7	100.0
Secondary evening schools	21.7	66.4	11.9	100.0
Continuation classes	62.8	20.9	16.3	100.0
Vocational schools	32.4	58.1	9.5	100.0
Agricultural schools	27.1	61.5	11.4	100.0
Teachers' training colleges				
1961/62	63.2	26.7	10.1	100.0
1966/67	61.0	33.0	6.0	100.0
1972/73	55.9	35.2	8.9	100.0

[1] Israel-born were classified by father's continent of birth—if the father was also born in Israel, they were included in the "Total" column only.
[2] Including pupils in classes without a clear grade.
[3] Excluding seminary classes in teachers' training colleges.

bodies facilitated speedy and diversified development. By 1972/73 there were 297 vocational postprimary schools in the state system, with almost 64,000 students, in which scores of subjects were taught in 12 basic curricula. In the late 1960s the ministry appreciably increased the funds allocated to vocational education and encouraged parents to send their children to such schools by introducing graded tuition fees for all pupils, whether or not they passed the *seker*. Two- and three-year vocational courses were also introduced into academic and comprehensive schools and some of them award a vocational matriculation certificate which paves the way for training as a technician or entry to the Technion.

The Ministry of Labor played an important role in the development of postprimary vocational education by the extension and diversification of apprenticeship programs. In 1973, 18,000 young people attended special courses for apprentices and youths, of whom 2,500 were being trained in industrial schools which combine vocational training and apprenticeship. The defense forces also established residential vocational schools for youths 16 years old and above, who continued their training during their period of military service. The vocational schools and some of the two-year schools in development areas were established on the joint initiative of public organizations, the Ministry of Education and Culture, and local authorities. A special impetus has been given to vocational education by the international organization ORT, whose network in 1973 included 70 schools with 35,000 students (including adults). The local authorities in cooperation with various bodies, the Amal network of the Histadrut, and various women's organizations, also ran vocational schools. Thirty to forty percent of the syllabus in vocational schools—about twice as much as in other countries—consists of academic subjects.

The Ministry of Education and Culture has devoted much attention to the adaptation of agricultural schools to technological developments. Courses and programs are diversified in content and standard so as to attract varied 37 types of students. The matriculation certificate in agriculture qualifies its holders for admission to the faculty of agriculture of the Hebrew University. Other incentives include graded tuition fees for all students and grants, where necessary, to cover fees in residential schools. There are 8,000 students in residential schools that have solved the problem of study away from home, which agricultural education generally involves. Another important factor in agricultural education is cooperation with the youth movements and the Gadna youth corps, both of which encourage settlement on the land. Twenty-six agricultural schools are inspected by the ministry; five of them are maintained by the state, while 20 were founded and are supported by public organizations, mainly Youth Aliyah and women's organizations. The syllabus includes both the humanities and the sciences and there are a variety of educational activities, especially in the residential schools.

Continuation (or extension) classes are to be found in 63 schools in kibbutzim and moshavim, with 7,000 students in 1972/73. These classes provide postprimary education for all children in the settlements up to the age of 18. Of the comprehensive curriculum, 28% is devoted to nature study and agricultural subjects. The aim of the educational policy is to bring up the new generation to settle on the land by treating the students as an integral part of the society and economy of the village. Maritime education and the training of fishermen has increased in recent years but still does not meet the demands for trained personnel made by the expanding shipping and fishing industries. Maritime schools had about 1,600 students in 1972/73.

The State Education law of 1953 allows for "recognized" schools which are not state schools. Agudat Israel runs the Independent Education system of recognized schools (Ḥinnukh Aẓma'i). In 1971–72 it comprised 125 primary schools—for boys and girls separately—with about 24,000 pupils, 6.5% of the primary school population. After the age of 14 boys go to yeshivot and girls to the Bet Ya'akov schools, 15 in number, which train kindergarten and school teachers. The state covers 85% of the system's educational budget, while additional subventions, as well as services, come from local authorities. The ministry's inspectorate is in contact with the management of the system, but it enjoys almost complete autonomy in the framing of its syllabus and the appointment of teachers. In practice, despite the extreme Orthodox objection to Zionist ideology, largely because of its secular elements, most of the Agudah schools have adopted Hebrew as the language of speech and instruction: a few still teach in Yiddish and are not recognized by the state. Pedagogic approaches and concepts have also changed under the influence of the realities of Israel life.

Apart from the recognized schools, there are *ḥadarim* (sing. *ḥeder*) and *talmud torah* schools, where only religious subjects are taught, with about 5,000 children of primary school age in 1967. In 92 yeshivot for youths of 14 to 18 there were in 1972/73 7,602 students and 4,383 in 15 vocational yeshivot for the same age group. There were 7,040

A *ḥeder* for Yemenite children in Jerusalem, 1950. Courtesy Jewish Agency Photo Service, Jerusalem.

students aged 18 to 22 in 70 higher yeshivot and 4,383 married students in 175 *kolelim*. Many of those institutions are residential and received pupils from abroad. These institutions receive partial support from the Ministry of Religious Affairs; some are supported by donors and organizations abroad, including the American Joint Distribution Committee. They have no contact with the Ministry of Education and Culture. (For further information see *Religious Life and Communities*.)

GENERAL SERVICES. Though the structure of the Ministry of Education and Culture provides for separate administrative and pedagogic services for primary and postprimary schools, the increasing interdependence of the two stages has led to a certain measure of integration in order to ensure continuity. The following are now common to both: (1) supplementary and social education; (2) the Jewish consciousness program; (3) pedagogical centers; (4) overhauling of curricula; (5) surveys and research.

(1) Supplementary education started with club activities in primary schools. In 1972/73 there were school clubs for 52,000 children; youth centers and community clubs for 66,000 youngsters, and technical clubs for over 2,500. These activities are generally started and supervised by local authorities. The ministry provides financial and organizational assistance to youth movements, which operate independently, in cooperation with schools. The Gadna program, in which the Ministry of Defense cooperates, includes excursions and physical training and encourages settlement on the land. On joining the army, many members of youth movements and Gadna opt for service in Naḥal groups, which combine military training with border settlement. The social education programs encourage active citizenship, the discussion of current affairs, publication of school newspapers, meetings between youth of different backgrounds, and participation in cultural and artistic activities and performances.

(2) Jewish conciousness. The object of the Jewish
40 consciousness program is to inculcate Jewish values and

A class in quality-control techniques at the Boys Town
Jerusalem religious technical high school. Photo Werner Braun,
Jerusalem.

impart a knowledge of Jewish practice and tradition. Three
two-year institutions for teachers provide a course of
studies including Talmud, *aggadah,* prayers and liturgical
hymns, Jewish thought, and problems of modern Jewry.
Conferences and discussions are held and teachers are
provided with guidance material.

(3) Pedagogic centers. In 23 centers of varying standards,
the teacher, especially the primary teacher, can acquire
educational aids, guidance material, and pedagogical
literature. The centers are also used for discussion and
study courses.

(4) Curricula. Eight units of the ministry have been
engaged in planning curricula, adapting them to changing
needs, providing teachers and pupils with up-to-date
textbooks and study aids, and utilizing experience gained
abroad. They pay particular attention to subjects such as
Jewish studies, English, and the sciences. To coordinate 41

their work, a curriculum center was established at the ministry in 1966. A Center for the Teaching of the Natural Sciences was also established, in cooperation with the Hebrew University and the Weizmann Institute. These programs have inaugurated regular cooperation with the teachers of the institutions of higher education.

(5) Surveys and research. The ministry conducts surveys and follow-ups, in particular with regard to subjects requiring special attention in primary education. Considerable funds are allocated for research projects, which are generally carried out by independent research bodies such as the Szold Institute, the Hebrew University's school of education, the departments of education at Tel Aviv and Bar-Ilan universities, and the Israel Institute of Applied Social Research. Some of these, notably the Hebrew University school of education, do research in connection with postprimary education on their own initiative.

Arab Education. Arab education in 1972/73 included 133,347 pupils, 14.5% of the total school population. Seventy-five percent studied in 338 state schools and the rest in other institutions, mainly community religious schools. Seventy-seven percent of the pupils were Muslims, 14% Christians, and 9% Druze. The distribution among the various types is shown in Table 2. When the Compulsory Education Law was passed in 1949, 50% of the boys of primary school age and 18.6% of the girls were at school. Many new schools have been opened since then and there is no Arab village or even Bedouin encampment without a school. In 1972/73, 95% of the boys and 80% of the girls of compulsory education age were at school. Attendance in the lower classes of primary schools is almost 100%, particularly in the Christian communities.

The increase in the number of pupils posed two urgent problems—buildings and teachers. Provision and maintenance of buildings is normally the duty of the local authorities, but there were few of these in the early years in the Arab areas, and it took time to organize them. There has been considerable progress in this domain, however, and the number of schools has been quintupled since 1948. In 1948 there were 352 classrooms for Arab students. Between 1948 and 1962, 1,168 new classrooms were built. Some 600 classrooms were built under the government's five-year development plan (1962/63–1966/67) for Arab areas and the second plan (1967/68–1971/72) provided for the construction of another 1,400. However, still further progress is required in the provision of buildings and equipment for both primary and postprimary schools.

In 1949, 90% of all Arab teachers were unqualified. In-service training courses were organized to enable teachers to prepare for qualifying examinations. In 1956 an Arab teachers' training college was opened in Jaffa and transferred to new premises in Haifa in 1964. It has 350 students, about half of whom come from villages and reside in the college. As a result of these measures, and despite the increase in the number of teachers (from 186 in 1949 to over 5,300 in 1972/73) almost half of them are now qualified. Two-thirds of the teachers are men. Textbooks have been published for primary school classes in all subjects and considerable progress has been made in the preparation of textbooks for postprimary schools. In 18 schools the grouping system has been introduced in Arabic and in arithmetic in the sixth and seventh grades. In 24 schools there is prevocational training. Radio and television broadcasts include special programs for Arab schools. The postprimary network is growing, though the local authorities are somewhat remiss in fulfilling their obligations. Thirty-five percent of the boys and 20% of the girls aged 14–17 attend school. The 23 vocational and agricultural schools are maintained mainly by the state and 10% of the Arab pupils receiving postprimary education study in Jewish schools.

The Arab schools inculcate Arab cultural and traditional values; the language of instruction is Arabic; Hebrew is taught from the fourth grade onward. Despite the progress that has been made and the cooperation of the Arab population, the question of identification with the State of

Elementary-school class in the Arab village of Bir al-Sheikh, early 1960s. Courtesy Government Press Office, Tel Aviv.

Israel remains an educational problem in Arab schools. Contact between Arab and Jewish pupils is limited, mainly because most of the Arab population is concentrated in its own villages and towns. However, there is a common scout federation; Jewish pupils taking oriental studies arrange visits and camps in Arab areas; there is a Friendship House in Haifa and similar institutions in several other places. Furthermore, the number of Hebrew-speaking Arabs is on the increase.

As a result of the Six-Day War (June 1967), the ministry and the military administration were faced with the responsibility for the education of 307,000 additional pupils, taught by 7,000 teachers in 900 schools, in East Jerusalem and the areas administered under the cease-fire agreements. There were 26,000 Arab pupils in East Jerusalem: half of them in government schools and half in private or community schools; with the reunification of the

Arab schoolboys in the workshop in the children's wing of the Israel Museum, Jerusalem. Photo Emka, Jerusalem.

city these schools became part of the municipal network. At first there was some opposition to the new situation on the part of the population, including teachers, but in a short time the schools were reopened and school life returned practically to normal. In accordance with the Compulsory Education Law, measures were taken for providing kindergarten schooling for children aged five. Responsibility for education in the administered territories in Samaria and Judea (the "West Bank"), the Gaza Strip, and the Golan Heights rested with the military administration in cooperation with representatives of the local populations. In these areas too, where there were 281,000 pupils, including 103,000 at schools run by the U.N. Relief and Works Agency, schooling returned almost to normal.

Teacher Training. In 1972/73, teachers numbered 44,186: 23,609 in primary schools and schools for handicapped children and 15,315 in postprimary schools and teacher-training colleges. Twenty-five percent worked part time. Primary school and training-college teachers are employed

45

by the government and postprimary teachers by local authorities or public bodies. In the years of mass immigration, which caused a rapid upsurge in the school population, half the teachers who were recruited were unqualified, having been given short, intensive preparatory courses before being sent to the classroom. The defense forces permitted girls to do their compulsory military service as teachers, especially in border settlements. Some of these went to teaching direct from the postprimary school; in other cases, military service was deferred to enable girls to take the regular training courses before taking up teaching posts. In 1967 1,246 army girls served in educational capacities in border settlements and development areas, many of them as counselors in youth clubs and in agricultural schools, or teaching illiterates. In 1967, 20% of primary teachers were unqualified, a quarter of these being regarded as incapable of passing qualification examinations. By 1970 the percentage of unqualified teachers had been reduced to 15.6%. Many postprimary teachers, too, are unqualified. In 1970, 47% had university degrees (only 57% of these with teaching diplomas); 21% (of whom 70% had pedagogical training) had an incomplete university education; and 32% (of whom 40% had primary-school teaching qualifications) had no academic education. In recent years there has been a decline in the demand for teachers, so that only qualified teachers were accepted for primary schools. In postprimary education there is still a shortage of graduate teachers with a teaching diploma. The feminization of the teaching profession continues. In 1970, men constituted 25% of primary and 51% of postprimary school teachers, but the percentage of male students in teacher training colleges was only 14. In the Arab training college the percentage was 58. The percentage of men among university students preparing for the teaching profession is well below the percentage of men teaching in postprimary schools.

Thirty-seven percent of the teachers came to Israel after
1948 and 40% were born in Israel. Sixteen percent of all

teachers are from Asia and Africa; their proportion will grow, as a third of the students in teacher training colleges came from these continents. The number of students in training colleges, which give a two-year course after matriculation, increased gradually to 7,500 in 1967, but fell to 5,100 in 1969/70. The increase in teachers' salaries in 1971 may raise recruitment to the profession. In 1963 the Dushkin Commission recommended, in order to raise the standards of teacher training, the consolidation of the numerous small training colleges into a smaller number of larger ones and the addition of a third year to the course of studies. Only a number of colleges have added the extra year; they admit graduates of others to complete their studies. Graduates of the three-year course are given the status of senior qualified teacher, with higher salary and other preferential treatment. However, the three-year course has put the universities into serious competition with the training colleges. In-service training courses assume various forms—some short-term, some lasting a year. Many of them are organized in conjunction with the Teachers' Association in Israel and the institutes of higher education.

Adult Education. Primarily concerned with the task of giving a basic education in Hebrew language and culture for new immigrants, adult education began with the First Aliyah and was greatly expanded when the Central Cultural Committee of the Histadrut was established during the 1920s. With the support of the Zionist Organization, it opened Hebrew courses and libraries all over the country. Other bodies working in the field were the local authorities, the Cultural Department of the Va'ad Le'ummi, and the Adult Education Center of the Hebrew University. When the State of Israel was established, Hebrew-language teaching for adults became the responsibility of the Ministry of Education and Culture and of the Jewish Agency, which together devised the *ulpan* scheme for new immigrants. The Histadrut and local authorities also participated on a smaller scale. The army set up its own

Ulpan class in Tel Aviv, 1967. Courtesy Government Press Office, Tel Aviv.

ulpanim for new immigrant soldiers, and helped the government to combat a new problem, that of illiteracy, created by the mass immigration of the 1950s. It assigned girl soldiers as teachers in outlying new settlements and towns in a massive campaign to teach reading, writing, and arithmetic to immigrants, mainly women, often in their own homes. The army also serves as an overall framework for primary and secondary education for thousands of immigrant soldiers, providing many of them with technical skills. The Jewish Agency publishes books and periodicals in simple vocalized Hebrew and the Histadrut publishes *Omer*, a daily newspaper in simple Hebrew. The Israel Broadcasting Service offers daily news and a program in simple Hebrew.

Other types of adult education are provided by the cultural departments of local authorities, the Histadrut, women's organizations, and political parties. They include

Army sergeant teaching new immigrants to read and write. Moshav Segullah, 1960s. Courtesy Government Press Office, Tel Aviv.

language courses, people's universities and high schools, evening courses for primary and secondary education, workers' schools, centers for further study in rural areas, university lectures, and tours to archaeological and historical sites. Kibbutzim, moshavim, homes for the aged, and rest homes also benefit from adult educational services. The Association for Adult Education coordinates activities and provides information and publicity. Learned societies, such as the Biblical Research Society, the Nature Preservation Society, and the Israel Exploration Society, are also active.

A specific aspect of adult education in Israel is religious study through talmudic discourses in synagogues, private study circles, and countrywide *yarḥei kallah* ("study months") when adults go to live and study at yeshivot. The revival of Hebrew has removed the language barrier from religious study, facilitating the inclusion of students hitherto not reached, including women. Weekly commentaries on the current portion of the Law are distributed. In addition to the Ministry of Education and Culture, many private bodies sponsor religious adult education, including synagogue associations, religious workers' unions, women's and youth organizations, and private societies formed for this purpose.

Since the establishment of the State of Israel, women's organizations have sponsored classes in reading, writing, and handicrafts for Arab women, and have provided them with domestic science courses, thus contributing to the rapid change in the status of women in Arab society. After the Six-Day War (1967), intensive courses in Hebrew were begun in East Jerusalem and the occupied territories, and many Jerusalem Arabs also study at *ulpanim*. The study of Arabic also became widespread, and spoken Arabic courses were initiated. Since the Six-Day War, Arabic has also been taught on the radio.

3 YOUTH MOVEMENTS

In Israel, as in some other countries, youth movements have passed through three major phases of development. The first was the romantic stage, in which they sought to develop their own distinctive culture, differing from that of the adults. Imbued with a rebellious idealism, the young people formed their own organizations and set themselves apart from the adult world. This was followed by the political stage, in which the movements no longer emphasized their separateness and strove to create their own culture, but saw it as their task to join the struggle to change society. The third was the realistic stage, in which youth movements became an established part of society, an educational agency like schools and extension courses. At this stage, although the romantic symbols were retained and the youth movements still took a stand on political issues, they had rid themselves of any rebellious tendencies and had simply become organizations of children and young people.

Pioneering Youth Movements. The pioneers of the Second Aliyah were mostly around the age of 20 and were motivated by a spontaneous revolt against the dominant tendencies in Zionism and Jewish life; they therefore fall within the category of the classical youth movement. They came as individuals and it was only after their arrival that they organized themselves into groups and took issue with the existing tendencies in the *yishuv*, protesting, for example, against the use of Arab labor, the prevailing tendency of assimilation to French culture, and the acceptance of the Uganda Scheme[1]. These protests contributed to the formulation of a new ideology, which regarded the worker's life as a national and social ideal and sought to make physical labor the highest social value. Similarly, in their initial stages the He-Ḥalutz movement[2] and the Gedud ha-Avodah (Labor Legion) of the Third Aliyah were also spontaneous developments dedicated to revolutionary aims and characteristic examples of a youth movement. They went a step further, however, by organizing as political bodies with the declared aim of achieving influence and determining the character of their society.

Ha-Shomer ha-Ẓa'ir (see below) in the Diaspora was also a genuine youth movement that passed through the romantic stage of a spontaneous search for new values to the formation of an autonomous public body. It introduced a new facet, however: the inclusion of children and adolescents in its sphere of activity, in order to indoctrinate them with the ideals of its founders and ensure the continuity of the movement and the maintenance of its ideals. In this respect, it might be said to have started on the road to the type of youth movement which is loyal to the aims of its elders.

At the beginning, the ideological ferment that the young people had brought with them from the Diaspora had no effect on the youth living in the country—either on the farmers' sons in the old moshavot during the Second Aliyah period or on the urban youth of the Third Aliyah period. Although a youth movement was established in Palestine in the early 1920s, it consisted of scout groups organized by the teachers, associated with the schools, and supported by the Jewish officials of the Mandatory government. It was an organization for youth, not a true movement, and had no ideology or political aspirations.

[1] The "Uganda Scheme," a proposal by the British Colonial Secretary, Joseph Chamberlain, in 1903, to make a region in what was to become Kenya an area for Jewish settlement. The scheme produced sharp controversy in the Zionist camp and was finally rejected in 1905.

[2] He-Ḥalutz ("The Pioneer"), a federation of pioneering Zionist youth movements active from the 1920s onward throughout Europe.

52

It was not until the late 1920s and 1930s, when the ideology of the labor movement had come to the fore and the *yishuv* had entered into a struggle for its physical existence and political future, that a true youth movement arose in Palestine. This was also the time when settlement on the land had become a vital necessity and the attainment of collective aims by *hagshamah azmit* ("personal fulfillment") was accepted as the *yishuv's* supreme task. The first halutzic movement of school youth, Ḥugim ("Circles"), was founded in 1927. At the same time there was a split in the Jewish scout movement, and in 1928 several scout groups joined with Ḥugim to form Ha-Maḥanot ha-Olim ("the Ascending Hosts"). The pioneering spirit also spread to Ha-No'ar ha-Oved, the organization of working youth, which had been founded in 1926 to protect wages and working conditions without stressing the duties of the individual and the personal obligation to realize revolutionary ideals. Toward the end of the 1930s the scout movement, modeled on the Baden-Powell pattern, was infused with the pioneering ideal, leading to national service and personal fulfillment in the kibbutzim.

From Youth Movement to Youth Organization. In order to achieve their aims and ensure the continuity of their settlement work, the founders of the youth movements had to develop a reservoir of young people to ensure continuity and bridge the gap between the generations. As a result, the youth movements turned into youth organizations affiliated with adult movements. This brought about significant changes in their character (although they continued to be called youth movements): the age limits were lowered to include nine- to ten-year-olds; the age at which members had to make a decision about joining a kibbutz was fixed at 18–20; an organized effort was made by the adult leaders to attract large numbers of children and adolescents to the movement and to inculcate them with ideals based upon the example of personal fulfillment set by the adults. Youth movement graduates from the kibbutzim served as instructors in town and country branches.

Badges worn by members of Israel youth movements. a.
Ha-No'ar ha-Oved ve-ha-Lomed. b. Israel Scout Federation.
c. *Benei Akiva.* d. *Ha-No'ar ha-Dati ha-Oved.* e. *Ezra.* f.
Betar. g. *Ha-Tenuah ha-Meuḥedet.* Courtesy Jewish Agency,
Jerusalem.

The change in the character of the movements in the
1930s and 1940s did not, however, lessen their practical
significance. The youth movements constituted an important factor in the political struggle of the *yishuv* for the right
to Jewish immigration, settlement on the land, and
self-defense. No longer in opposition, the youth movements, in their new form, were a product of the existing
society, concentrating their activities on the agricultural
labor settlements, which had become the example of the
54 *yishuv's* ideals, while their members modeled themselves on

the kibbutz pioneer, with his social prestige, and tried to follow in his footsteps. In addition to their primary task—to provide a permanent reservoir of manpower for the kibbutzim—the youth movements also had a lasting effect upon those of their members who did not join a kibbutz; these continued to accept the supremacy of the kibbutz ideal, even though they themselves had not lived up to it. Thus they performed the function of cementing the bonds between the kibbutz movement and society as a whole.

The Jewish youth movement in Palestine developed a special type of youth culture, standing halfway between conformity and revolt. They accepted the society's ideals, but called for their immediate personal fulfillment; they may have appeared to be in opposition to society, suspicious of it, even rebellious; in fact, however, they accepted the prevailing ideal—that of a pioneering society—and were only impatient with the gap between ideal and practice. Organizationally, they also combined opposing trends: they had formal patterns of activity and maintained national secretariats, but they had no permanent staff: the instructors *(madrikhim)* generally came from their own ranks—often from the movement's kibbutzim—and served for relatively short periods. Though the movements stressed their independence, they were, in fact, closely linked to adult organizations, such as labor federations, political parties, and agricultural settlement movements.

From the Establishment of the State (1948). The position of the youth movements and the outlook for their development in the future have been affected in various ways by the changes that have taken place in independent Israel. First, the appearance of normalcy was created, as though the time had come to follow the pattern of long-established nations. Second, the great mass of the new immigrants, with their tradition of the family as the center of social life and their unfamiliarity with socialist and pioneering ideologies, could not settle down in the kibbutzim. Third, the modernization of the economy and the need to utilize scientific methods called for specialization, advanced training, and higher education. The result was a rise in the status of the academic professions, the senior civil service, and the higher ranks in the army, to the detriment of the kibbutz ideal, which lost much of its attraction.

The members of the youth movements felt that they were being trained for tasks and ways of life that no longer represented the central needs of Israel society. In the 1950s there was a crisis in the youth movements, and many of the adolescent members fell away. The competition between the movements for the allegiance of the children was criticized as introducing politics into the educational system, and, except for the non-party Scouts, they were not permitted to operate in the schools.

Ultimately, however, it began to be widely realized that Israel was still in need of strong youth movements, for a variety of reasons: the slackening of ideological fervor among the population as a whole enhanced the importance of an educational framework based on voluntary fulfillment of ideals; the growing formality and authoritarian discipline of the school system increased the need for a more spontaneous form of education, based on voluntary adhesion and independent effort, in which the instructor would be more like an elder brother than a teacher; the country still needed volunteers to settle in the large unpopulated areas of the country, for only a thriving and prosperous countryside could guarantee the territorial basis of sovereign independence; the kibbutz had a special role to play in facilitating economic advance without enlarging social antagonisms and promoting the dispersal of the population. These were some of the considerations which, in 1959, induced the Israel government to institute cooperation between the state educational system and the youth movements and permit them to recruit members in the state schools (see below).

In the 1960s the youth movements reexamined their basic

Two founder-members of the Naḥal settlement of Gerofit, November 1963. Courtesy J.N.F., Jerusalem. Photo A. Strajmeyster, Jerusalem.

principles in the light of changes that had taken place in the country and, in particular, in the kibbutz movement, which no longer banned higher education or training for the professions and provided opportunities for highly skilled work in agriculture and in the modern industries to be found in many kibbutzim. Whereas in pre-State days groups of youth movement graduates joined the Palmaḥ [3]

[3] Palmaḥ (abbr. of *peluggot maḥaz*, "shock companies"), elite troops of the Haganah Jewish underground forces in Ereẓ Israel, established in 1941 and disbanded by the Israel Defense Forces in 1948.

and combined agricultural settlement with military training, today they serve in Naḥal, establishing and maintaining security settlements. On completion of their military service, they may help to turn the settlement into a civilian village, join another one, continue their studies, or take up the vocation of their choice. Service in Naḥal, followed by permanent settlement in kibbutzim, has thus become the main goal of the pioneering youth movements. They have also carried out various tasks in the new-immigrant villages and development towns—especially among children of parents from Muslim countries—organizing youth clubs, raising the level of political awareness, and helping to form settlement groups.

In general, the movements constitute a framework for social contact; a natural background for meetings between boys and girls; a means of enhancing the social status of the members; a channel for the communication of information, attitudes, and norms useful for integration in society; an instrument for fostering ideals and devotion to national goals; an organization for voluntary activities for the benefit of new immigrants, slum dwellers, etc.; and an auxiliary organization for the kibbutz movement. In the early age-groups these aims go hand in hand, but incompatibilities arise later, resulting in a larger number of dropouts in the higher age-groups. Most of the movements maintain contact with Zionist or general Jewish youth movements abroad.

Youth Movements and their Affiliations. There are 11 youth movements in Israel, and all, except the Scouts, are affiliated with adult organizations. The largest is Histadrut ha-No'ar ha-Oved ve-ha-Lomed (the Federation of Working and School Youth, founded 1924), affiliated with the Histadrut. It operates not only as a youth movement, with its educational activities and its close association with the kibbutzim founded by its graduates, but also as a junior trade union organization, helping to improve wages, working conditions, and facilities for vocational training. Working closely with Iḥud ha-Kevuẓot ve-ha-Kibbutzim

Watchtower at a scout camp in Jerusalem, 1957. Courtesy Jewish Agency, Jerusalem.

and Ha-Kibbutz ha-Me'uḥad (two organizations of collective villages), Ha-No'ar ha-Oved recruits most of its instructors and youth leaders from the Israel Labor Party. It is associated with the world movement of Iḥud Habonim (Heb. *Ha-Bonim*, "The Builders") first established in Great Britain in 1929.

Next comes Histadrut ha-Zofim be-Isra'el, the Israel Scout Federation (established 1919; reformed 1936), an apolitical body that operates under the aegis of the Ministry of Education and Culture, which appoints half the members of its governing body. While emphasizing kibbutz settlement, it trains its members for national service as well as pioneering, and seeks close cooperation with parents and schools. It has both religious and general sections and has affiliated Arab and Druze groups, in addition to Jewish groups; it maintains ties with the Shaḥar (formerly Young Judaea) movement abroad and with the international scout movement.

The third in size is Benei Akiva ("Sons of Akiva," founded 1929), the largest religious pioneering movement, whose Israel Organization is affiliated with Ha-Kibbutz ha-Dati (in whose kibbutzim its graduates play a prominent part) and the National Religious Party and has close ties with the Torah ve-Avodah ("Law and Labor") movement in the Diaspora. Other religious youth movements are Ha-No'ar ha-Dati ha-Oved (Working Religious Youth), affiliated with Ha-Po'el ha-Mizrachi and similar in its activities to the Working and Student Youth, and Ezra, which is attached to Agudah's labor offshoot, Po'alei Agudat Israel.

The more left-wing kibbutz organizations are represented by Ha-Shomer ha-Za'ir ("The Young Guard," first established 1913), affiliated with Ha-Kibbutz ha-Arzi and the Mapam party, and Maḥanot ha-Olim ("The Camps of the Ascenders," established 1927; see above), affiliated with Ha-Kibbutz ha-Me'uḥad. The former is part of the world movement of the same name, while the second is associated with the Deror movement abroad. Both are very closely bound to their parent bodies and are marked by strong political motivations.

On the center and right wings of Israel politics are: Ha-No'ar ha-Oved ha-Le'ummi, (National Working Youth), affiliated with Histadrut ha-Ovedim ha-Le'ummit, a non-Socialist labor movement; Maccabi ha-Za'ir (Young

Maccabi), which lays emphasis on sports and is sympathetic to the Liberal Party; Betar (abbr. of *Berit Yosef Trumpeldor*, "The Joseph Trumpeldor League;" established 1923), which is associated with its parent movement in the Diaspora and the Ḥerut Movement in Israel; and Ha-Noʻar ha-Ẕiyyoni (Zionist Youth; established in Poland in 1938), associated with Ha-Oved ha-Ẕiyyoni and the Independent Liberal Party, as well as the movement of the same name abroad.

Table 6. Members of Youth Movements—1973

Working and School Youth	106,000
Benei Akiva	25,500
Federation of Scouts	25,000
Betar	15,000
Ha-Noʻar ha-Dati ha-Oved (Working Religious Youth)	14,500
Ha-Shomer ha-Ẕaʻir	13,000
Working National Youth	12,000
Maccabi ha-Ẕaʻir	8,000
Ha-Noʻar ha-Ẕiyyoni	6,600
Ha-Maḥanot ha-Olim	4,500
Ezra	3,500
Total	233,600

There are four types of groups in the movements: educational groups of young people whose parents belong to the settled town population; young people living in the new-immigrant villages and development towns; trade union sections of working youth; and young people in the moshavim and kibbutzim. The Federation of Working and Student Youth comprises all four types; the other movements contain one or more in various proportions.

State and Public Support. The youth movements receive guidance and support from the Ministry of Education and Culture and the Youth and He-Ḥalutz Department of the World Zionist Organization. The ministry's budget for the work totaled about IL2,000,000 in 1972/73 to cover the cost of camping grounds and equipment, publications, film strips and slides, seminars for youth instructors, field study centers, building and maintenance, etc. The movements are represented on the Council of Youth Movements under the auspices of the Zionist Organization's Youth and He-Halutz Department, which conducts the Institute for Israel Youth Leaders; has a library of films, phonograph records, etc. on loan; holds seminars and study courses; and advises the movements in planning their activities. The council also acts as the Israel secretariat of the World Union of Jewish Youth and appoints Israel's representatives at the meetings of the World Association of Youth.

4 HIGHER EDUCATION

Institutions. The idea of establishing a university in Jerusalem was first mooted late in the 19th century by Zionist leaders who believed that it could not only absorb Jewish students barred from East European universities, but also contribute to the development of the Land of Israel as the spiritual center of the Jewish people. In 1901 a proposal to explore the possibilities of founding such an institution was submitted to the Fifth Zionist Congress, but it was not until 1913 that the 11th Zionist Congress resolved on immediate practical steps toward the establishment of a

The Mount Scopus campus of the Hebrew University of Jerusalem.
Photo Werner Braun, Jerusalem.

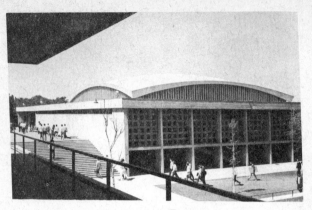

The Churchill Auditorium at the Technion, Haifa. Photo Keren-Or, Haifa.

Hebrew university in Jerusalem. Activities in this direction began immediately, but were interrupted by the outbreak of World War I.

The foundation stones of the Hebrew University were laid on Mount Scopus in 1918, even before the conclusion of the war, and the official opening took place in 1925. The war also delayed the opening of the Haifa Technical Institute (now the Technion—Israel Institute of Technology), the establishment of which had begun in 1913, so that it was able to admit its first students only at the end of 1924. The growth of both institutions was slow at first, but their development was accelerated after the rise of Hitler in 1933, when the influx of Jews from Central Europe brought not only a larger number of students, but also scholars and scientists who joined their academic staffs. On the eve of the establishment of the State of Israel, the Hebrew University had about 1,000 students and the Technion over 700.

Higher education has expanded tremendously since the establishment of the state to meet the urgent needs of a rapidly expanding and developing society. Not only has the number of students at the Hebrew University increased

Library building of Tel Aviv University. Photo Israel Sun, Tel Aviv.

more than fifteenfold and at the Technion about eightfold, but five additional institutions of higher education have been established: the Weizmann Institute of Science at Reḥovot, Tel Aviv University, Bar-Ilan University, the University of Haifa, and the University of the Negev in Beersheba (renamed after David Ben-Gurion in 1973).[1] The municipality of Ḥolon, near Tel Aviv, has taken the first steps toward the establishment of a technical college. By 1973, an academic staff of 7,600 taught over 50,000 students in Israel's seven universities. Higher education has thus expanded at a much higher rate than the population as a whole. The number of high school graduates increased annually and more and more were eager to obtain a university education. The country's rapid economic development required a constantly growing number of persons with academic and technological training, while the expanding state services called for an ever increasing supply of university-trained civil servants.

In 1973 the Hebrew University of Jerusalem had an enrollment of 17,500 students in seven faculties—humanities, social sciences, science, law, agriculture, medicine (including pharmacy and dental medicine)—and in schools and institutes for education, social work, librarianship, Asian and African studies, international relations, Jewish studies, home economics, applied science, technology (graduate school opened in 1970), etc. There were also centers for pre-academic studies (with over 1,000 students) and for documentation and research in connection with Soviet and East European Jewry. The university's academic staff, many of whom are its own graduates, numbered over 1,800. Deprived of access to its Mount Scopus buildings in 1948, the university built a large new campus on Givat Ram in western Jerusalem. Following the reunification of the city in 1967, the university started to rebuild and extend its original campus, and its academic activity is now conducted in four centers: Mount Scopus, Givat Ram, the Medical Center at Ein Kerem, Jerusalem, and the Faculty of Agriculture in Reḥovot. It has conferred over 25,000 degrees.

In the 1950s the Haifa Technion broadened its original objective of training engineers and architects to include teaching and research in mathematics, physics, and chemistry; it also included general courses in humanities and languages for all students. In 1973, it had over 8,000 students in 18 faculties and departments, with about 1,300 professors and lecturers.

The Weizmann Institute of Science at Reḥovot, founded in 1949, whose main activities are in the field of research, inaugurated in 1963 the Feinberg Graduate School, which had an enrollment of about 600 doctoral and Master of Science students in 1973/74. In 1973 the Institute acquired a $2.7 million IBM computer and dedicated an observatory for geophysical research near Eilat.

Tel Aviv University, established in the 1950s by the municipality of Tel Aviv, has developed into an autonomous institution receiving municipal support. In 1973 it had about 15,000 students, with an academic staff of 2,036, in faculties of humanities, natural sciences, medicine, continuing medical education, law, and arts and communications; a department of education; an academy of music; schools of business administration, social work, and communication disorders; a technical college; a technological center;

The Erna and Jacob Michael Institute of Nuclear Science at the Weizmann Institute, Reḥovot. Photo Ben-Zvi, Rehovot.

and 29 research institutes.

Bar-Ilan University, Ramat Gan, founded by the Mizrachi Organization of the U.S. in 1955, places special emphasis on Jewish tradition and Jewish studies, all students being required to take courses in Bible and Talmud. In 1973 it had nearly 6,000 students, with an academic staff of some 900, in faculties of Judaic studies, language and literature, humanities and social sciences, and natural sciences and mathematics, as well as schools of education and social work and an institute of criminology. Bar-Ilan set up various extension courses and opened an institute for research into Eastern Jewry, housed in the Old City of Jerusalem.

The University of Haifa, set up by the municipality in 1963 as Haifa University College under the academic supervision of the Hebrew University, had 3,600 students in 20 departments in the humanities and social sciences, with 527 teachers, in 1973. In 1969 the Haifa municipality took the first steps toward the establishment of a medical school with the initiation of clinical courses at local hospitals for fourth-year students.

Table 7. Students and Recipients of Degrees in Academic Institutions (1948/49–1970/71)

	1948/49	1950/51	1956/57	1960/61	1967/68	1970/71
Students	1,635	3,022	5,842	10,836	28,520	40,087
First year students	405	1,085	1,770	3,296	7,740	9,480
Research students	88	148	343	516	1,208	1,729
Recipients of degrees	193	313	884	1,654	3,761	6,451
The Hebrew University[1]						
Students	957	2,068	3,666	7,020	11,586[2]	13,962
First year students	215	799	1,112	2,096	2,746	2,853
Research students	86	146	306	431	767	1,026
Recipients of degrees	58	125	536	1,004	2,160	2,901
Technion—Israel Institute of Technology						
Students	678	954	2,004	2,380	5,115	6,922
First year students	190	286	658	541	947	(1,200)
Research students	2	2	37	85	189	358
Recipients of degrees	135	188	348	591	815	1,120
Tel Aviv University						
Students	——	——	——	825	6,308	8,978
First year students	——	——	——	378	1,864	2,410

Research students	—	—	—	—	12	—	1,219
Recipients of degrees	—	—	—	23	421	—	—
Bar-Ilan University							
Students	—	—	—	172	611	3,111	4,775
First year students	—	—	—	—	281	1,176	1,226
Research students	—	—	—	—	—	8	47
Recipients of degrees	—	—	—	—	36	204	716
University of Haifa							
Students	—	—	—	—	—	1,829	3,087
First year students	—	—	—	—	—	815	950
Research students	—	—	—	—	—	61	365
Recipients of degrees	—	—	—	—	—	—	—
University of the Negev [3]							
Students [3]	—	—	—	—	—	264	1,834
First year students	—	—	—	—	—	192	841
Recipients of degrees	—	—	—	—	—	—	55
Weizmann Institute of Science							
Students	—	—	—	—	—	307	529
Research students	—	—	—	—	—	232	298
Recipients of degrees	—	—	—	—	—	100	75

[1] Including Tel Aviv Branch (since 1959/60). [2] No new students were admitted in the Tel Aviv Branch; since 1965/66 to the Social Sciences faculty and since 1966/67 to the Law faculty. [3] Students of the Institute for Higher Education in the Negev, who studied for the M. Sc. degree in Engineering were included with the Technion.

Table 8. Academic Staff in Academic Institutions 1948/49–1971/72

	1948/49	1950/51	1956/57	1960/61	1967/68	1971/72
The Hebrew University						
Academic staff	208	278	638	925	1,371	1,711
Professors and lecturers	98	116	185	338	908	1,221
Technion—Israel Institute of Technology						
Academic staff	85	114	456	434	863	1,325
Professors and lecturers	20	22	207	195	416	634
Tel Aviv University						
Academic staff	—	—	—	136	1,312	2,036
Professors and lecturers	—	—	—	55	498	786
Bar Ilan University						
Academic staff	—	—	40	107	454	868
Professors and lecturers	—	—	—	35	309	390
University of Haifa						
Academic staff	—	—	—	—	216	527
Professors and lecturers	—	—	—	—	71	192
University of the Negev						
Academic staff	—	—	—	—	169	673
Professors and lecturers	—	—	—	—	72	252
Weizmann Institute of Science						
Senior academic staff	—	—	—	—	114	175

The campus of Bar-Ilan University, Ramat Gan. Photo Werner Braun, Jerusalem.

The University of the Negev, Beersheba, established in 1965 as the Institute for Higher Education in the Negev under the supervision of the Hebrew University, the Technion, and the Weizmann Institute, has degree courses in the humanities, social sciences, natural sciences, and engineering. In 1973 it had an enrollment of about 2,800 and an academic staff of 673, many of them part-time.

Organization and Administration. Israel's institutions of higher education are autonomous bodies with their own boards of governors to look after finance and development and (with the exception of those affiliated to other universities) their independent academic authorities. Their organizational structure is, to a large extent, modeled on that of the Hebrew University, which is described below. Supreme authority is vested in the board of governors, composed of distinguished academics and public men from all parts of the world. The board, which meets once a year, exercises ultimate control in matters of major policy, 71 approves the annual budget, and authorizes the establishment or abolition of faculties and departments on the recommendation of the senate and executive council. The board appoints the president of the university, who is the head of the administration, and the vice-presidents. Between meetings of the board of governors, an executive council, with both academic and nonacademic members, is responsible for the conduct of university affairs subject to the board's overriding powers. Day-to-day affairs are dealt with by the permanent committee appointed by the executive council, which has a majority (roughly two-thirds) of nonacademic members. The supreme academic body of the university is the senate, which enjoys academic autonomy. It is composed of the deans of the faculties, all full professors, and representatives of other academic ranks. The chairman of the senate, the academic head of the university, is the rector, who is elected by the senate from among the full professors. A small standing committee, including the rector and the deans, deals with matters preparatory to their discussion by the senate and also transacts business which is not dealt with by the senate as a whole. Within each faculty, academic matters are dealt with by a faculty board, which elects the dean. The rector is an *ex officio* member of each such board. Academic appointments and promotions are decided upon by special committees, the composition and functions of which are prescribed by the senate, the executive council, and the board of governors.

Finance. Until the mid-1950s all but a small proportion of the maintenance and development costs of the universities was covered by contributions from individuals and societies of "friends" abroad, together with students' fees; government grants, to subsidize current expenditures, were small. Development needs were met almost entirely by donations from Jews abroad, usually for the establishment of specific buildings, departments, or institutes, named after the donors or their relatives. Owing to their rapid expansion, however, their financial needs grew continuous-

Table 9. Participation of Public Sector in General Budgets of Institutions of Higher Education (in IL million)[1]

	1957/58		1963/64		1966/67		1968/69		
	B	G	B	G	B	G	B	A
Technion	6.3	2.0 (32)[2]	15.6	8.5 (55)	31.8	20 (63)	41.5	29.1 (70)
Hebrew University	10.5	4.3 (41)	23.6	17.7 (67)	58.1	35 (60)	74.3	51.8 (70)
Weizmann Institute of Science	4.3	1.1 (26)	11.4	2.5 (22)	21.2	7.8 (37)	25.3	15.8 (62)
Bar Ilan University			2.8	0.7 (25)	8.5	3.9 (46)	13.5	9.0 (66)
Tel Aviv University			3.5	0.7 (20)	20.2	8.0 (40)	41.0	23.0 (56)
Haifa University			1.5	0.1 (7)	4.5	1.4 (31)	6.6	3.7 (56)
University of the Negev					0.9	0.7 (77)	2.9	2.1 (72)
Totals	21.1	7.4 (35)	61.1	30.2 (50)	145.2	76.8 (53)	205.1	134.5 (65.5)

[1] Legend: B—Budget, G—Government participation. A—Jewish Agency participation.
[2] Figures in brackets are percentages of the budget.

73

Table 10. Estimates of Accumulated Capital Investments in Israel's Institutions of Higher Education[1] and Means Used to Finance Them

	Cost	% Government	% Gifts	% Loans
Technion	IL 85 million	27	60	13
Hebrew University	$ 110 ,, [2]	10	76	14
Weizmann Institute of Science	$ 100 ,,	12	65	25
Bar Ilan University	IL 19 ,,	12	70	18
Tel Aviv University	IL 75 ,,	23	38	39[3]
Haifa University	IL 6.5 ,,	25 [4]		

[1] As of March 31, 1969.
[2] Includes buildings under construction, exclusive of the Mt. Scopus development program.
[3] Includes loans and deficits.
[4] The other 75% came from the Haifa Municipality.

ly, and so did government assistance. State grants covered 35% of the total current outlays of the institutes of higher learning in 1957/58 and 53% in 1966/67. There was also more support from individuals and institutions in Israel.

While the Six-Day War was followed by a vast increase in the burden of defense on the state budget, the growth in the immigration of young people from Western Europe and the Americas led to heavy pressure on the facilities for higher education, which also became an important stepping-stone toward settlement in the country. Although the government continued to provide modest subsidies—mainly, now, for development costs—the greater part of the financial responsibility was taken up by the Jewish Agency, through its Emergency Appeal for Israel. Government allocations totaled IL24,700,000 in 1969/70 and IL38,500,000 for 1970/71, while the Jewish Agency subsidies for the same years amounted to IL171,400,000 and IL212,000,000, respectively. About 70% of the aggregate maintenance budgets of the universities is now covered from public funds. This increased financial dependence may lead to pressure for greater public control.

The Teaching System. The teaching system in Israel's universities represents a mixture of the European and American systems. The European system, which is based on lectures given by teachers with the students as passive listeners taking down notes, was brought over by the first university teachers, virtually all of whom came from Eastern and Central Europe, and it prevailed exclusively for many years. In time, however, many of the graduates of the Hebrew University, and later also of the others, carried out postgraduate studies in the United States and on taking up academic posts in Israel introduced certain American methods of teaching. This process was further stimulated by the increasing number of Americans who joined the faculties. As a result there is now greater interaction between teachers and students, with more discussion and many more seminars supplementing formal lectures. These changes have been most marked in the social sciences.

The European system, however, is still dominant and it has given rise to considerable discontent on the part of the students, who have felt that the professors and lecturers are out of touch with their problems. In general, the students feel they should have some say in academic affairs; at the Hebrew University they demanded representation in the senate. The authorities at some universities took steps to deal with these grievances. They set up joint teacher-student committees in some departments so that the students' point of view could be heard and their problems could be taken into account when academic matters were under consideration.

The Student Body. In 1948, there were two institutions of higher learning in Israel, with 300 professors and lecturers serving some 1,600 students. In 1973 there were seven with an academic staff of some 7,600 and a student population of about 50,000 (including over 9,000 from abroad and about 700 Arabs). In 1965, according to UNESCO figures, for every 100,000 of the population there were 1,700 students in Israel institutions of higher learning (including non-degree-granting institutions), compared with 480 in Britain, 598 in Egypt, 1,042 in France, and 2,840 in the United States.

Students of both sexes and of all races and creeds are eligible for admission to Israel's institutions of higher learning, but the vast majority are Jews, most of whom were born or received their schooling in Israel. About one-third are women. With few exceptions, Israel students enroll after having completed their military service, which means that they are generally some years older than students elsewhere. While at the university they suffer considerable hardship through the interruption of their studies by service in the reserves, for which they are called up at frequent intervals and for extended periods, with the result that some have to devote more than the minimum number of years prescribed in order to qualify for their degrees. Since they have reached an age where they are reluctant to be dependent on their parents, who are generally not in a position to support them, a high proportion—about 70–80%—have to work either part or full time to maintain themselves while studying.

The universities try to alleviate the difficulties of their students in various ways: by offering loans, scholarships, and fellowships—contributed mainly by the Israel government and sympathizers in Israel and abroad—the number of which, however, is still not sufficient; by supporting student cafeterias where meals are served at modest prices; and by building dormitories where students can live and study in comfort at reasonable cost. The rapid increase in the student population in recent years has highlighted the need for many more dormitories, and considerable efforts are being made to provide them. This is especially true of the Hebrew University, whose extensive development program includes dormitory facilities on the Mount Scopus and Givat Ram campuses and in various suburbs of Jerusalem. In the academic sphere there are problems of a different kind. Since much of the required reading, including textbooks, appears in languages other than Hebrew, the student must devote time to a study of foreign languages for professional purposes; at some universities a preparatory course in English is compulsory. The high cost of books also constitutes a problem, particularly as the universities cannot afford to stock their libraries with a sufficient number of copies.

The percentage of the student body (not counting foreign students) who belong to the oriental communities (i.e., are of African or Asian origin) has grown from 6% in 1957/58 to 13% in 1972/73, but it is still too low. This is part of the basic problem of fully integrating immigrants of all origins and their children into the life of the country; the immediate cause is the imbalance which exists in the academic high schools, from which most university students come. In the latter years pupils born in, or whose parents came from, African or Asian countries made up only 32% of the enrollment in these schools, compared with 58.1% in vocational high schools and 61.5% in agricultural schools.

The Hebrew University, the Technion, and the University of the Negev hold special intensive seven- to eight-month courses, with the cooperation of the Israel Defense Forces, to enable young men, mainly from the oriental communities, to begin preparing for their university studies while they are still in the army.

The students' own organizations carry out a variety of cultural, social, and aid activities. The oldest is the Hebrew University Students' Organization, which, inter alia, runs a labor exchange to help students find employment and assists them to obtain living accommodation and interest-free loans. It also maintains a cooperative bookshop and publishing service, which supplies students with texts and stationery at reduced prices, and prints authorized lecture notes and even textbooks in Hebrew. All the students' organizations are affiliated to the National Union of Israel Students, whose governing bodies are elected by secret ballot. However, campus student activities are less intense and varied than in many other countries.

Students from Abroad. Since the end of World War II, when about 100 students from English-speaking countries enrolled at the Hebrew University, most of them American ex-servicemen benefiting from the G.I. Bill of Rights, there has always been a sprinkling of overseas students at Israel's universities, and after the early 1960s their numbers grew. Non-Jewish as well as Jewish students from abroad began making their appearance on the campuses, the former including scores from the newly emerging states on the African and Asian continents. The largest project inaugurated for the benefit of students from the developing countries was that undertaken by the Hebrew University-Hadassah Medical School, which between 1961 and 1966 ran a special medical course for them, instruction in the preclinical stage being given in English. Seventy students took advantage of the course. The number of Jewish students from abroad grew steadily, but slowly, over the years, but after the Six-Day War it increased at an

unprecedented rate. In 1973 it reached a figure of over

9,000, some enrolled in regular courses and others in special ones organized for them. About 7,000, who came as immigrants or potential immigrants from 63 countries, received aid and financial services from the student authority under the auspices of the Ministry of Immigrant Absorption and the Jewish Agency's Immigration and Absorption Department. More than half of those assisted studied at the Hebrew University, 11% at the Technion, 10% at Tel Aviv, 9% at Bar-Ilan, and about 3% at the University of the Negev, the remainder being at the Weizmann Institute, Haifa University, and other institutions. The institutions devote special attention to the academic and social needs of students from abroad: they hold Hebrew-language courses mainly for their benefit: and some courses are also given in English.

Israel Students Abroad. In 1970 about 7,000 Israel students, at a rough estimate, were pursuing their studies abroad, some two-thirds of them in the United States. Most of them had already taken a first degree in Israel and left to obtain more advanced qualifications. Others went abroad because they had failed to gain admission to certain local faculties with limited capacity, such as medicine, or wanted to pursue their studies in fields not available in Israel, such as certain marine or veterinary sciences. Taking into account the fact that a student's stay abroad is sometimes prolonged in order to obtain a second degree or acquire practical experience in his field, it is estimated that about 80% of them ultimately come back. The Ministry of Labor has a special department to find posts for them and facilitate their return.

Council for Higher Education. In 1958 the Knesset passed a law setting up a Council for Higher Education, headed by the minister of education and culture and comprising 23 members, the majority of whom are appointed in consultation with the recognized institutions of higher education. The functions of the council are to grant recognition to institutes of higher learning on the basis of prescribed rules and appropriate scientific standards, but subject to appeal and the approval of the government; to withdraw such recognition; to approve what academic degrees may or may not be conferred by each institution and on what conditions; to make proposals for the development of existing institutions and the establishment of new ones; and to advise the government on its financial assistance to the recognized institutions. The law stresses the freedom of opinion and conscience enjoyed by the institutions and emphasizes that the council may not limit these freedoms in any manner or form. Every recognized institution is at liberty to conduct its academic administrative affairs, within the limits of its budget, as it deems fit. In view of the accelerated expansion of higher education, the growing need for coordination, and the increased pressure for financial support by the state, the minister of education and culture foreshadowed in June 1970 the introduction of legislation to amend the powers and composition of the council, which would, inter alia, provide for the appointment of a Universities Grants Committee on the British model.

5 INSTITUTIONS OF HIGHER LEARNING

Hebrew University of Jerusalem. The establishment of an institute of higher learning in Ereẓ Israel was first proposed by Hermann Schapira[1] in 1884 at the Kattowitz conference of the Ḥovevei Zion, and again at the first Zionist Congress in 1897. A few years later, a group of young Zionists were inspired by Chaim Weizmann[2], then a teacher at the University of Geneva, to make the foundation of such an institution a primary aim of the Zionist movement. The group, which included Martin Buber[3] and Berthold Feiwel[4], brought the question before the Congress of 1901, and Herzl submitted a petition to the Ottoman sultan for permission to establish a university in Jerusalem.

The Congress of 1913 appointed a committee, including Weizmann and Judah L. Magnes[5] of America, to execute the project, but the outbreak of World War I prevented action. While the war with the Turks was still being waged, Weizmann, who had come to Ereẓ Israel as head of the

[1] Prof. Hermann Ẓevi Schapira (1840–1898), rabbi, mathematician, and Zionist leader, also advocated the establishment of the Jewish National Fund.

[2] Dr. Chaim Weizmann (1874–1952), chemist and Zionist leader, became Israel's first President in 1948.

[3] Martin Buber (1878–1965), an intellectual leader of the German Zionists, gained a worldwide reputation as a religious philosopher and joined the Hebrew University's faculty in 1938.

[4] Berthold Feiwel (1875–1937) was one of the major Zionist personalities of Western Europe.

[5] Judah Leon Magnes (1877–1948), an American Reform rabbi and Zionist, became chancellor of the Hebrew University (1925) and, from 1935, its first president.

Chaim Weizmann and General Allenby at the foundation-stone ceremony of the Hebrew University of Jerusalem, 1918. Courtesy Hebrew University, Jerusalem.

Zionist Commission after the issue of the Balfour Declaration, initiated the establishment of the university. On July 24, 1918, 12 foundation stones of the university were laid on Mount Scopus, north of the Old City of Jerusalem. This site, incomparable in beauty and impressiveness, had been acquired before the war by the Jewish National Fund from the estate of an English lawyer, Sir John Gray-Hill. The view commanded on one side the Holy City and Bethlehem, and on the other the rugged landscape of the Wilderness of Judea, the Jordan Valley, the Dead Sea, and the Mountains of Moab. Weizmann, the only speaker at the ceremony, concluded: "Here, out of the misery and the desolation of war, is being created the first germ of a new life . . . In this university we have gone beyond restoration; we are creating during the war something which is to serve as symbol of a better future. In the university the wandering soul of Israel will reach its haven."

There was an interval of seven years before any faculty of the university could be opened. The first lecture was given in 1923 by Albert Einstein on his theory of relativity, and he spoke the first sentences in Hebrew, which was to be the language of teaching. He was dedicated to the university, and had accompanied Weizmann to the United States in 1921 to apprise American Jewry of its significance. It was decided that, before undergraduate teaching was initiated, work should be in postgraduate studies and scientific research. Three tiny institutes of research were opened, in Jewish studies, chemistry, and microbiology. The university was to develop in two directions: on the one hand, it should be the center where the Hebrew tradition would be molded in its original language and in the light of general humanities; on the other, it should be a center of research in the natural and medical sciences, which would help the regeneration of the land. The former development was the work of Magnes, who settled in Jerusalem in 1923, and devoted himself to bringing the university into being. Weizmann and committees in England and the United States launched the effort for scientific research. The university was opened on April 1, 1925, by Arthur Balfour[6], at an impressive ceremony attended by the High Commissioner, Sir Herbert Samuel, General Allenby, Chaim Weizmann, H. N. Bialik, Aḥad Ha-Am, and Chief Rabbi Kook.

The university did not at that time receive any grant from the Government of Palestine; it was the financial responsibility of the Jews of the world. The supreme governing body included Jews eminent in public or academic life in many countries. Weizmann was chairman of the board, and Magnes chancellor—later president. The university grew quickly. In addition to the Institute of Jewish Studies (1924), two other Institutes were established following the inauguration: chemistry and microbiology. These were followed by

---

[6] Arthur James, Lord Balfour (1848–1930), the British statesman who, as Foreign Secretary in Lloyd George's war cabinet, issued the Balfour Declaration favoring "the establishment of a Jewish National Home" in Ereẓ Israel (1917).

oriental studies (1926); mathematics (1927); general humanities (1928); philosophy and history, geography and archaeology, classical literature, English, and other languages; physics (1930); and biological sciences (1931). Demand grew for regular courses of undergraduate studies, leading to a Master's degree. Two faculties were constituted: Humanities and Science and Mathematics. The first degrees were awarded in 1931. At this stage, however, the authorities were opposed to the opening of professional schools for doctors or lawyers; learning should be acquired for its own sake, and research was the main objective. About half the students were from Palestine, and half from abroad. Some of the teachers now appointed were graduates of the university.

The Nazi persecution of Jews in Germany and their

Official opening of the Hebrew University by Lord Balfour, April 1, 1925. Seated at the table are (left to right) the Sephardi chief rabbi, Yaakov Meir, the Ashkenazi chief rabbi, Abraham Isaac Kook, Lord Allenby, Sir Herbert Samuel, Dr. Chaim Weizmann, and the British chief rabbi, Dr. J. H. Hertz. Courtesy State Archives, Jerusalem.

exclusion from institutions of higher learning gave fresh importance to the Hebrew University. It could take its part in the battle for academic freedom, and be a principal place in which exiled scholars and scientists could find a haven. Hebrew remained the language of instruction, and was rapidly adapted to the needs of modern learning and science. Vocabulary, based on biblical and rabbinical Hebrew, multiplied. The collection of the Jewish National and University Library, housed in the Wolffsohn Building, grew to half a million books, and contained one of the most valuable collections of Hebraica and Judaica. By 1973 the Library, now located on the Givat Ram campus, contained over 2 million volumes and 25,000 periodicals. Before the outbreak of World War II, medical research was developed in laboratories attached to the Hadassah University Hospital, and both the hospital and medical center did valuable work for the Allies and the civilian population of the Middle East throughout the war. By 1948, in addition to the three initial institutes, the university comprised the faculties of humanities and science, the pre-faculty of medicine, the school of agriculture, the department of education, the Hebrew University Press (now the Magnes Press), the Jewish National and University Library, the Museum of Jewish Antiquities and the Museum of Biblical and Talmudic Botany and Jewish and Arab Plant Lore. The University grew from a faculty of 33 and a student body of 164, in 1925, to a faculty of 190 and a student body of 1,027, in 1948. By 1973, the university had a student body of over 18,000 and a faculty of 1,800, many of whom are graduates of the Hebrew University.

With the formal establishment of the State of Israel on May 14, 1948, a full-scale war erupted. The approach to Mount Scopus passed through the Arab quarter of Sheikh Jarrah, from where Arab snipers attacked vehicles en route to the university and to the Rothschild-Hadassah University Hospital. As the result of an attack on April 13, 1948, in which 77 persons were killed, the university was forced

Administration building on the Givat Ram campus of the Hebrew University of Jerusalem. Photo David Harris, Jerusalem.

to suspend its activities on Mount Scopus. Although Mount Scopus was declared a demilitarized area several months later, access to it by the Jewish population was limited to a specified number of civilian caretakers, who were placed fortnightly under U.N. supervision. All efforts to effect normal access to the university failed, and for the next 19 years the university on Mount Scopus remained empty.

On April 22, 1949, the new academic year opened in the rented premises of the former college attached to the Franciscan Monastery of Terra Sancta in Jerusalem, as well as in other buildings scattered throughout the city. The following 15 years were notable for the large-scale development of the university: the school of agriculture became a full faculty in 1952; in 1958 the newly-built campus at Givat Ram was dedicated. During this period the faculties of medicine, dental medicine, law, and social sciences were established, as were the graduate library school, the school of pharmacy, and the Paul Baerwald School of Social Work. In 1963, the new Hebrew University-

Hadassah Medical School was inaugurated in the Jerusalem suburb of Ein Karem.

To assist those students unable to study in Jerusalem, the university established extension courses in other parts of the country and assumed responsibility for the academic development of Haifa University. The University, together with the Technion and the Weizmann Institute of Science, also shares responsibility for the academic growth of Ben-Gurion University in Beersheba. The University receives the combined financial help of the state and of Jewish communities and individuals abroad. Government and Jewish Agency grants cover nearly two-thirds of the maintenance budget; and societies of friends of the university have given the funds for new buildings. The university has not, however, become a state institution. The government attaches no conditions to its contribution, has no administrative control, and nominates only a few lay members to the executive council. The university is open to all students without discrimination of sex, creed, color, or nationality. The number of students from abroad steadily

Bar Aton, the university's student club at Givat Ram.

mounted, and there was a large influx of Jewish students, most of them American, after the Six-Day War. In 1973, foreign students totaled 4,000. In addition, 205 were Arabs or Druze (45), including some from East Jerusalem and the Israel-held territories in Judea and Samaria.

The Board of Governors, meeting annually in Jerusalem, elects the president for a four-year term, approves the budget, and decides major issues of policy. Half the board consists of members resident in Israel. The control of the university is maintained by a senate, an academic body presided over by an elected rector, and an executive council, composed of a majority of lay members together with some academics. After Dr. Magnes, the presidents were: Prof. Selig Brodetsky (1949–51), Prof. Benjamin Mazar (1953–61), Prof. Giulio Racah (acting: 1961–62), Dr. Eliahu Elath (1962–68), and Avraham Harman (from 1968). Following the reunification of Jerusalem in June 1967, the university embarked on an extensive building development program on Mount Scopus. Presently located in new or renovated buildings are the faculty of law, the Institute of Archaeology, the School for Overseas Students, First-year Science Studies, the Center of Pre-Academic Studies, the Authority for Research and Development, The Harry S Truman Research Institute, and dormitory facilities for approximately 3,000 students. When completed, the Mount Scopus campus will also include the faculties of humanities and social sciences, the School of Education, the Martin Buber Adult Education program, a central library, student center, sports facilities, faculty club, and administration building. With university activities once again centered on Mount Scopus, the Givat Ram campus will be used primarily for expansion of the teaching and research programs in the natural and experimental sciences.

Technion, Israel Institute of Technology. Israel's oldest engineering university, is situated in Haifa. Paul Nathan of Berlin, one of the leaders of the Hilfsverein der Deutschen Juden, was the father of the plan for a technical school in Haifa. Aided by a 100,000 ruble gift from the heirs of Kalonymus Wissotzky of Moscow and a $100,000 contribution from Jacob Schiff of New York, the Hilfs-verein proceeded to construct a building, with Alexander Baerwald as architect. The cornerstone was laid on the slopes of Mt. Carmel in 1912. Zionist personalities sat on the governing board, in addition to leaders of the Hilfs-verein.

As the date approached for the opening of the school, then known by the German name Technikum, a struggle broke out in the governing board over the language of instruction. The Zionist minority insisted on Hebrew, but the majority voted for German. The decision aroused a storm of controversy, in which the Hebrew Teachers' Association took the lead. Meetings were held throughout the country; resolutions of protest were passed by practical-ly all Jewish institutions and organizations; the Teachers' Association issued a ban against the acceptance of posts or the registration of students at the Technikum; pupils at the Hilfsverein's other schools struck in support of a demand to institute Hebrew as the sole language of instruction, and many of the teachers resigned. This "language conflict" helped to accelerate the establishment of a network of national Hebrew schools. The opening of the Technion was delayed and, before the controversy could be settled, World War I broke out. The unoccupied building served as a military hospital, first for the Turkish forces and later for the British. After the war, the Zionist Organization acquired the property from the Hilfsverein and the first classes on a university level were held in December 1924.

In the period preceding the establishment of the state, and especially during the administration of Shlomo Kap-lansky as head of the institution (1931–50), the school developed as a technological university training engineers on Central and Eastern European standards. Yaakov Dori, who was president from 1951 to 1965, with the assistance of Sydney Goldstein, who was vice-president for some years, altered the educational patterns of the Technion, modeling it more on similar institutions in the

United States. In addition to the faculties of engineering and architecture, a faculty of natural sciences and mathematics was opened in 1953. In 1952 the Technion began conferring masters' and doctors' degrees, in addition to those of bachelor and ingénieur. A school of graduate studies was formally established in 1957. In 1953 the Technion began its move from the original building in midtown Haifa to a 300-acre campus on Mt. Carmel, popularly known as Technion City. Dori was succeeded as president by Alexander Goldberg in 1965 and Amos Horev in 1973.

The following faculties and departments exist at the Technion: Aeronautical Engineering, Agricultural Engineering, Architecture and Town Planning, Chemical Engineering, Chemistry, Civil Engineering, Electrical Engineering, Food and Biotechnology, General Studies, Industrial and Management Engineering, Materials Engineering, Mathematics, Mechanical Engineering, Mechanics, Nuclear engineering, Physics, and Teacher Training. Ancillary units include the Technion Research and Development Foundation Ltd., established in 1952, and the Junior Technical College, founded as a technical high school in 1933.

Research is carried on in all faculties and departments. Of special interest is the work done in water desalination, medical electronics, construction methods, farm machinery, aerodynamics, and hydraulics. Projects are sponsored by industry, the government of Israel, and foreign governments and foundations through the Research and Development Foundation, which had a turnover of IL28,000,000 in 1972/73. The foundation operates field laboratories and offers consultant services, testing facilities, quality control, and technological surveys. In 1973 the academic staff numbered about 1,500 and there were over 10,000 students, including 3,000 in the graduate school, as well as 1,709 in the Junior Technical College, 2,788 in the School for Senior Technicians and over 11,000 in extension courses in various parts of the country. By 1972 the Technion had granted almost 12,000 bachelors degrees, about 1,900

Campus of the Technion, Israel Institute of Technology, Haifa.
Photo Keren-Or, Haifa.

masters degrees, and 490 doctorates; 2,516 graduates had
been granted the diploma of ingénieur. The Technion is
an independent institution under the authority of its board
of governors, which includes civic and industrial leaders,
representatives of the teaching staff, the alumni, the
government, and Technion Societies in various parts of
the world. It is recognized for the conferment of academic
degrees by the Israel Council for Higher Education. The
executive body is the council, which meets monthly, and
the chief executive officer is the president, appointed by
the board of governors. Academic authority is vested in
the senate, composed of the president, the vice-presidents,
all full professors, and other representatives of the academic staff. The operating budget of the Technion for 1972/73 was
IL100,000,000 of which Jewish Agency and government
participation covered approximately 65%, the balance
coming from contributions, tuition fees, and commissioned
research.

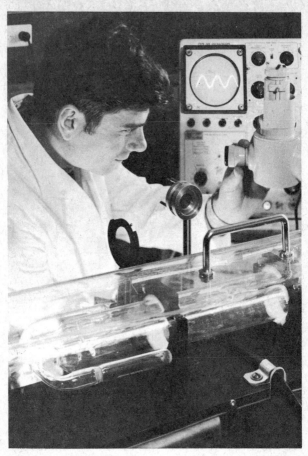

Advanced research on lasers in a laboratory at the Technion.
Photo Keren-Or, Haifa.

Weizmann Institute of Science. The Weizmann Institute
developed out of the Daniel Sieff Research Institute,
founded in Reḥovot in 1934 with the aid of the Sieff
family (of England), which had a staff of ten scientists,

Opening of the Daniel Sieff Research Institute, the precursor of the Weizmann Institute of Science, Reḥovot, 1934. The speaker is Yiẓhak Wilkansky (later Elazari-Volcani), and at his left are the high commissioner, Sir Arthur Wauchope, and Chaim Weizmann. At far left is Arthur Ruppin. Courtesy Yad Vashem Archives, Jerusalem. Photo Orient (Z. Kluger), Tel Aviv.

headed by Dr. Chaim Weizmann, and ten technicians. When the Weizmann Institute of Science was established in 1949, it consisted of nine departments with a scientific staff of 50, including research students. In 1973 the Institute community numbered about 2,100, including some 470 full-time scientists and over 600 students at its Graduate School.

The Institute is administered by a Board of Governors and an Executive Council. It is headed by a President and helped by a Council of Deans. The Scientific Council advises on matters of academic policy, appointments, and promotions. The Institute consists of 19 research departments, grouped in five faculties: Biology (Cell Biology, Biological Ultrastructure, Biodynamics, Genetics, Plant Genetics and Chemical Immunology), Biophysics and Biochemistry (Biophysics, Biochemistry, and Polymer

Research), Chemistry (Organic Chemistry, Structural Chemistry, Isotope Research, Chemical Physics, and Plastics), Mathematics (Applied Mathematics and Pure Mathematics), and Physics (Nuclear Physics and Electronics). The Science Teaching Department is represented on the Council of Deans by the Dean of the Graduate School. The Presidents of the Institute have been: Chaim Weizmann (1949–52); Abba Eban (1956–66); Meyer W. Weisgal (1966–69); and Albert B. Sabin (1970–72); and Israel Dostrovsky (1973–   ). Weisgal was named Chancellor in 1970.

The first major building of the enlarged Institute, planned in 1944 as a 70th birthday gift for Dr. Weizmann, was dedicated in 1949. The principal scientific structures on the campus in 1973 were the Jacob Ziskind Building, the Wolfson Institute of Experimental Biology, the Erna and Jakob Michael Institute of Nuclear Science, the Levine Institute of Applied Science, the Ullmann Institute

The original building of the Daniel Sieff Research Institute, designed by Benjamin Chaikin. The bronze sculpture in the foreground, by Nathan Rapaport, was dedicated in 1969 in honor of Lord Sieff's 80th birthday. Photo Ben Zvi, Reḥovot.

of Life Sciences, the Institute of Biodynamics, the Daniel Sieff Research Institute and the Institute of Organic Chemistry, the Dannie N. Heineman Accelerator Laboratory, and the Animal Breeding Center.

Weizmann Institute scientists are engaged in some 400 research projects on subjects such as cancer research, immunology, elementary particle physics (both experimental and theoretical), solid-state physics, seismology, and computer design and construction, as well as those indicated by the names of the departments.

Research on biological problems is carried out on three levels: the molecular, the cellular, and the level of organisms. Work has been done on the synthesis of proteins and nucleic acids and the way in which the genetic code directs this synthesis; synthetic polypeptides; biochemical reactions produced by light radiation; the structure and function of antibody molecules; antibody and antigen interactions, and other immunological phenomena. On the molecular level, Institute scientists are working on the analysis and control of cell differentiation and the immunological tolerance of cells; the inhibition of spontaneous and induced leukemia; the replication of tumor cells and the causes of carcinogenesis. Research is also being carried out on the physiology of reproduction.

In 1967 the Institute built its second electronic computer, the Golem[7] A and is now completing work on Golem B. Computers are used by scientists in all departments, the applied mathematicians employing them in the study of earthquakes, ocean tides, and the flow of viscous fluids. The Applied Mathematics department also investigates problems in terrestrial atomic spectroscopy and has helped to locate underground fuel and water reservoirs. The Institute's physicists have made important advances in their efforts to analyze the properties and structure of nuclei and elementary particles, supported by a Tandem van de

[7] This Hebrew term, meaning a "shapeless mass" (cf. Psalms 139:16), was applied in kabbalistic legend to some clay monster brought to life in defense of the Jews by wonder-working.

Graaff accelerator and, for the analysis of bubble chamber photography, by a novel television measuring projector designed and built on the campus. Particularly well known is their theoretical work on nuclear structure, higher symmetries, and many-body problems. Other areas of investigation include magnetism, solid state physics, and chemical physics. Fundamental research in chemistry is carried out in many departments. The Chemistry Departments proper are engaged in projects which range from aspects of photochemistry to the chemistry of natural products (such as those found in medicinal plants and in the spinal cord); the structure of solids, crystals, and other chemical compounds; and the synthesis of compounds of industrial importance. The Polymer Department deals with giant molecules, such as those which form membranes, both natural and synthetic, that can be used in the separation of salts from water. In the Isotope Department, Institute scientists work primarily on the way in which chemical reactions take place—from simple gas reactions of the upper atmosphere to complex biological processes in bone and brain. They are also involved in the environmental sciences through the investigation of the natural water cycle, which is of the greatest importance to Israel and many other countries short of water.

The Yeda Research and Development Company, owned by the Yeda Trust, deals with the commercial promotion of some of the more industrially promising research projects developed at the Institute, mainly in the fields of chemicals, electronics, pharmaceuticals, and plastics. Science-based industries have been set up in the immediate vicinity of the Institute.

Weizmann Institute scientists are involved in revision of methods for teaching the natural sciences in Israel, the supervision of some programs on educational television, and the direction of science summer camps at the Institute for high school students from Israel and abroad. They also act as advisers to local industry and to various ministries.

The Institute attracts many foreign scientists (as many as a hundred a year work in its laboratories for varying periods of time), and has become a meeting place for international scientific conferences and for the Reḥovot Conferences, at which leading statesmen and administrators from developing countries meet to discuss specific subjects with distinguished world scientists. The first Reḥovot Conference in 1960, presided over by Abba Eban, was devoted to science in the advancement of new states. Subsequent gatherings were: Comprehensive Planning of Agriculture, 1963; Fiscal and Monetary Problems, 1965; Health Problems, 1967; Science and Education, 1969: Urbanization and Development, 1971: and Economic Growth in Developing Countries, 1973. Institute expenditure (about IL65 million in 1970/71) is covered mainly by research grants from overseas scientific agencies, by public funds, and by private donations. The Weizmann Institute has contributed considerably to the growth and development of the State of Israel and has enhanced the country's contribution to international scientific research.

Tel Aviv University. The name Tel Aviv University was first established in 1956, but the antecedents of the institution go back to 1935, when the Tel Aviv School of Law and Economics was established. In 1953 and 1955 the Tel Aviv municipality founded University Institutes of Biological Studies and of Jewish Studies, which in 1956 referred to themselves as faculties of Tel Aviv University. In the late 1950s the Tel Aviv School of Law and Economics became a branch of the Hebrew University faculties of Law and Economics. In 1965 this branch together with the faculties of Biological and Jewish Studies were combined into Tel Aviv University, first as a municipal institution and, from 1962, as an autonomous body, supported by the municipality, the government, and friends in Israel and abroad. The new university grew rapidly from about 1,650 students in 1962/63 to some 15,000 in 1973, with an academic staff of over 2,000. It tries to meet the urgent needs for higher education of the populous and developing area in which it is situated and enables many teachers and others in employ-

Campus of Tel Aviv University. Photo Israel Sun Ltd., Tel Aviv.

ment to undertake part-time studies. Up to the end of 1970 it had awarded 2,994 degrees.

In 1970 the university comprised faculties of humanities, with 22 major departments—seven in Jewish fields and 15 in general humanities; science, with ten major divisions: physics and astronomy, botany, zoology, biology, microbiology, mathematical sciences, chemistry, biochemistry, environmental sciences, and engineering sciences; social sciences, including sociology, political science, developing countries, economics, statistics, and labor studies; accountancy; law, inaugurated in 1966; continuing medical education, offering courses once or twice a week for physicians and dentists; a medical school, which opened in 1965 with courses for fourth- and fifth-year students and inaugurated a full six-year course; a graduate school of business administration, opened in 1967; a department of education, offering training for secondary school teachers; an academy of music, which offers a comprehensive musical education and trains music teachers; and a school of social work. A new faculty of arts and communications, covering, *inter alia*, musicology, theater arts, films, and television, was opened in 1972. There are 37 research institutes, includ-

Table 11. Tel Aviv University by Field of Study (1970–71)

	Humanities	Social Sciences	Law	Medicine	Sciences	Business Administration	Academy of Music	School of Social Work	Total
Academic Staff	641	225	71	298	669	50	38	27	2,019
Professors and Lecturers	356	90	40	293	372	32	34	20	1,237

	Humanities	Social Sciences	Law	Medicine	Sciences	Business Administration	Department of Education	Academy of Music	School of Social Work	Special Courses and Programs and Students Completing Degrees	Total
Students	3,216	2,162	1,157	885	1,531	433	306	145	114	2,592	12,541
Research Students	34	1	—	9	170	—	—	—	—	—	214

ing the Rogoff Institute for Medical Research (at Beilinson Hospital); the Donolo Institute for Physiological Hygiene; the Tel Hashomer Institute of Human Genetics; the Chaim Weizmann Institute for Zionist Research (jointly with the Jewish Agency); the Reuben Shiloah Center for Middle Eastern and African Studies; and institutes for research on planetary and space science, nature preservation, problems of the Diaspora, archaeology, Hebrew literature (Benzion Katz Institute), urban and regional studies, and human genetics. Research equipment includes a CDC 6600E control data computer, the largest of its kind in the country, and an astronomical observatory at Mizpeh Ramon.

The university's campus at Ramat Aviv comprised some 25 buildings in 1971, representing an investment of over IL130,000,000, mostly contributed by donors from abroad, especially from the U.S. The budget for 1970/71 (excluding development) was IL66,000,000, of which 70% came from the government of Israel and the Jewish Agency, and IL3,000,000 from the Tel Aviv municipality. The university has a board of governors and an executive board and council, of which Mordekhai Namir, former mayor of Tel Aviv, was chairman. George Wise was president of the university from 1963; in 1971 he became chancellor and Yuval Neeman president. The senate, headed by the rector, supervises all academic affairs, elects the rector and the vice-rector, and approves appointments of deans (who are elected by the faculty councils) and of the senior academic staff.

Bar-Ilan University. Founded in 1955, the university has as its purpose the advancement of knowledge in both Jewish studies and general science and research in accordance with the ideology of *Torah im Derekh Erez* ("Torah with general knowledge"), which led to the foundation of similar institutions in the Diaspora, such as Yeshiva University in New York. In the late 1940s a plan evolved to establish a religious university in Erez Israel was supported by the Mizrachi movement in the United States. The idea received further impetus under Pinkhos Churgin's leadership in the U.S. Located on a site east of

Ramat Gan, the university was named for Meir Bar-Ilan[8]. At the outset, the Bar-Ilan project received little encouragement in Israel. The government doubted the need for a university in addition to the Hebrew University in Jerusalem. Agudat Israel and similar Orthodox groups were fearful of imperiling certain types of religious education, particularly the yeshivot. However, it gradually became clear that there was a need for extending and diversifying higher education in Israel. The first president of the university was Pinkhos Churgin (1955–57), its founder. In 1957 Joseph Lookstein was appointed chancellor. Under Lookstein's leadership the university grew rapidly and received a charter from the state of New York. The first academic year began with 80 students and 19 lecturers. In 1973 the University had about 6,000 students and almost 900 lecturers, with more than 800 foreign students. Bar-Ilan is modeled on the American university pattern, which follows a credits system. The compulsory basic study of Jewish subjects includes Bible and Talmud. University studies are divided into three stages: the B.A. in humanities and B.S. in sciences, which require a four-year study period, as against three years in other institutions in Israel; the M.A. or M.S.; and the Ph.D. Instruction and research are carried out within separate faculties for Jewish studies, languages and literature, humanities and social studies, and science and mathematics. The university also has a criminology institute and a school of social work, whose students receive a B.S.W. at the end of their course. There are also university extension courses at Ashkelon (begun in 1965), Safed (begun in 1968), Afulah and the upper Jordan Valley (begun in 1972). An institute for research into Eastern Jews and their culture, housed in the Old City of Jerusalem, was opened in 1972. The university campus covers 270 dunams, with 20 buildings. Dormitories provide housing for 300 students, with an additional 500 units

[8] Rabbi Meir Bar-Ilan (Berlin: 1880-1949), the son of a foremost Lithuanian talmudist, was an author and editor; he became president of the World Mizrachi movement of religious Zionists.

planned. The university publishes the *Bar-Ilan Annual, Studies in Judaica and the Humanities*. It is administered by a senate, comprised of the deans and representatives of the professors, and lecturers, and the Board of Trustees, which includes religious and civic leaders and scholars from Israel and the Diaspora.

University of Haifa. The establishment of a Haifa university college in 1963 was the result of a growing demand for such an institution in northern Israel and negotiations between the Haifa municipality and the Hebrew University of Jerusalem. The municipality assumed administrative responsibility for the college, while the Hebrew University provided academic guidance and supervision. In 1970, the college changed its name to the University of Haifa and, two years later, it was granted full academic autonomy by the Council for Higher Education. Owing to the proximity of the Technion, Haifa University has concentrated on the humanities and social sciences (which are taught in the two major faculties), but there are also schools of education and social work, a center for maritime studies, and the beginnings of a medical school. By 1973, the University of Haifa catered for some 3,600 students and had a faculty of over 500 teachers. The Ohel Sarah College of the Emek and the Oranim Teachers' College are now branches of the University of Haifa.

Ben-Gurion University of the Negev. When the original Institute for Higher Education in the Negev opened at Beersheba in 1965, it enjoyed the distinction of being the first center of academic study planned by the Israel government to promote regional development. The University of the Negev, renamed Ben-Gurion University of the Negev in 1973, was initially supervised by the Hebrew University, the Haifa Technion, and the Weizmann Institute of Reḥovot. Although several departments deal with the humanities, the major emphasis has been placed on the natural sciences and engineering, no less than 85% of the academic staff teaching these subjects. One of the university's principal aims is to attract new immigrants with high intellectual and cultural attainments to the Negev region so as to create a productive society based on sophisticated and technological economy. Full accreditation was granted in 1969 and increasing self-sufficiency is now becoming evident. The Negev Institute for Arid Zone Research (founded 1958) was incorporated into the university in 1972 and a medical school is in process of formation. By 1973, there were 2,850 students, the teaching faculty of 673 including many professors and lecturers "on loan" from the Hebrew University.

Part Two:

SCIENCE IN ISRAEL

1 PRE-STATE BEGINNINGS

For newly independent Israel—poor in natural and material resources—scientific research, rapid industrialization, and technological development constituted the major hope for economic progress and the successful absorption of mass immigration. Israel was not unprepared. During the half century between the First Zionist Congress and the establishment of the state in 1948, the tradition of Jewish scholarship, the determination to transform the barren and often disease-ridden wastes of the country into a modern state, and, above all, the nature of Zionist ideology were driving forces which created functioning, institutionalized bases for modern scientific research, technological achievement, and the training of a new generation of scientists. Two of the country's major scientific institutions, the Hebrew University of Jerusalem (which began with three modest institutes of chemistry, microbiology, and Jewish studies) and the Technion—Israel Institute of Technology, Haifa, were established almost a quarter of a century before the state itself came into being.

At the beginning of the 1900s, the idea to found an institution for technical education had come from Dr. Paul Nathan of the Hilfsverein der Deutschen Juden. With money donated by the heirs of K.Z. Wissotzky of Moscow and Jacob Schiff of New York, the foundations of the Technion in Haifa were laid (see above, Chap. 5). The institute was formally opened in 1924 for the training of engineers.

In 1923, a host of over 150 illustrious Jewish scholars from many nations contributed as authors or editors to the publication of *Scripta Universitatis atque Bibliothecae*

Hierosolymitanum in fields of Jewish scholarship as well as the physical and biological sciences. This publication, founded and financed by Simon Velikovsky and edited by his son Immanuel, heralded the opening of the Hebrew University in 1925 (see above, Chap. 5). On the editorial board were world-ranking scholars such as Einstein, Hadamard, Landau, Levi-Città, Loew, and Wassermann. In 1938 they also published *Scripta Academica Hierosolymitana*, which strove to gather research scientists to pave the way for the establishment of an academy of sciences.

The Daniel Sieff Research Institute, where Chaim Weizmann had his laboratory, was established in 1934 among the orange groves in Reḥovot, next to the Agricultural Research Station. Weizmann was particularly keen to produce petroleum substitutes through the fermentation of agricultural products. The synthetic oil industry was to free the great powers of the Western world from dependence on the Middle East. In 1944, to commemorate Weizmann's 70th birthday, friends began the expansion of this institute into the Weizmann Institute of Science, which was opened in 1949 (see above, Chap. 5).

Love of Labor and Agriculture. Whereas cultural and spiritual values were an ideal of the Jewish people, the return to work on the land was an integral part of the Zionist ideology. Some of those who zealously adhered to the latter even negated the Jewish yearning for scholarship and believed only in the "religion of labor." However, a combination of both strivings is found in agricultural teaching and research. Before the end of the 19th century, the Mikveh Israel Agricultural High School was founded. In the early 1900s, agricultural experiments took place in Baron Edmond de Rothschild's settlements, and in 1906 Aaron Aaronsohn established an agricultural research station at Athlit which was the first research institute in Erez Israel. Aaronsohn made an important contribution to science when he discovered wild wheat growing in Rosh Pinnah, which led to a deeper understanding of cultivated wheat.

In 1911, Prof. Isaac Elazari-Volcani (Wilkansky) began experiments on his training farm in Ben Shemen, and in 1921, together with Prof. Otto Warburg, he established the Experimental Agricultural Station (Institute for Agriculture and Natural Sciences) for the Zionist Organization. This was transferred to the Government in 1951, and is now called the Volcani Institute of Agricultural Research.

These institutes and stations, backed by ideology, promoted cooperation and understanding between farmers and agricultural research workers, and have been instrumental in making agricultural products the most important export of Israel today.

Medicine. The first medical services were initiated in 1912, before World War I, with the founding of the Hebrew Health Station by the philanthropist Nathan Straus, and the Pasteur Institute by Dr. Arieh Beham. Yet even before this, there were dedicated pioneer physicians such as the "doctor of the settlements," Dr. Hillel Joffe.

The Institute of Microbiology (Parasitology), founded in 1924 by the Hebrew University, and the Departments of Biochemistry, Bacteriology, and Hygiene (headed by Professors Adler, Fodor, and Olitzki) established in 1926, were the basis of a medical center which the Hadassah Organization started to plan in 1927. In that year, Profs. Kliegler and Mer founded the Malaria Research Station in Rosh Pinnah. Out of these beginnings were to emerge the Prefaculty of Medicine, founded by Hadassah in 1939, and the Medical School ten years later.

Industry. Industrial research was pioneered by the Palestine Potash Company, which utilized the only raw material of substantial proportions in Erez Israel. In 1930, the Dead Sea Laboratories, founded by Moshe Novomeysky and headed by Dr. R.M. Bloch, began to work in close cooperation with the Hebrew University.

Governmental Science Prestructures. In 1921, the British Mandatory Government established the Central Government Laboratories for Public Health, followed by a meteorological service (1937), a forestry station, a veterinary (1925), a hydrological institute (1931), and a building testing station which later became the Standards Institution of Israel. The Board for Scientific and Industrial Research (BSIR) was the successor of the Scientific Advisory Committee of the Palestine War Supply Board, formed in 1942 to promote the Allied war effort. The BSIR was the predecessor of today's National Council for Research and Development. Thus the State of Israel had a scientific establishment long before a political one came into being.

2 AFTER THE ESTABLISHMENT OF THE STATE

When the State of Israel was established in 1948, three full-fledged academic institutions were already in existence—the Hebrew University, the Technion, and the Weizmann Institute of Science. There were also Government, public, and private research institutes. Two thousand students were taught by an academic staff of 300. The number of scientists in the natural sciences, engineering, agriculture, and medicine (SEAM) engaged in teaching, research, and development did not exceed 400.

Since then, viewed through the development of universities, governmental and public institutions, private industry, and defense, scientific work has doubled every five years.

Universities. Whereas in 1948, 2,000 students were taught by an academic staff of 300 in three institutions, there were in 1973, after 25 years, seven universities, with a student body that had grown 25-fold to over 50,000 and an academic staff of 7,600 (see Chaps. 4 and 5, above). These numbers also include the humanities and social sciences, but even taking only the number of students, teachers, and publications in the natural sciences, engineering, agriculture, and medicine, this growth pattern still applies. The proportion of students in the population who pursue higher learning has risen from 1,700 students/ million population to 17,000/million (Tables 1, 2, 3).

Industrial Research. No comparable zooming rate of growth has taken place in the industrial applied science sector, but research utilizing the most valuable human resource of know-how was to compensate for the lack of

Table 1. Growth of Science in Israel, 1928–1973

	1929	1939	1949	1959	1967	1973
Institutions of higher learning						
Number	2	2	3	5	7	7
Staff	80	—	300	1,490	3,750	7,610
Staff in Natural Sciences	—	—	—	—	—	4,286
Students in Natural Sciences	370	1,300	2,000	9,800	25,540	50,000
Ph.D.s awarded in Natural Sciences	0	6	10	91	123	220
No. of Agriculture and Engineering Research Institutes	4	5	14	32	54	60
Research Scientists in Nat. Sci., Med., Eng., and Agr.	80	—	400	1,400	2,841	7,000
Publications in Nat. Sci., Med., and Eng.	75	127	250	—	2,000	—
Jewish Population in Israel (in thousands)	174	450	1,179	2,088	2,657	3,000
GNP[1] (IL million at 1971 prices)	—	—	1,100	3,150	5,560	23,000
R & D[2] expenditure as % of GNP (incl. defense)	—	—	—	1.1	2.1	2.4[2]
Students/million population	213	3,000	1,700	4,900	9,210	17,000

Based on Shaul Katz: *The Growth of Science in Israel.*

[1] GNP: Gross National Product.

[2] As compared to Belgium 1.1, France 1.9, Germany 1.6, Greece 0.2, Holland 2.1, Italy 0.7, Japan 1.5, Norway 0.8, Spain 0.2, Sweden 1.6, UK 2.6, USA 3.6 (Ben Porath, in: *Science Policy*, ed. Tal and Ezrahi, 1972).

natural resources by establishing sophisticated science-based industries.

Table 4 shows that, as in 1950, the picture of the inverted pyramid still persists. As opposed to developed countries, in Israel an overwhelming percentage of scientists is engaged by academic institutions (65%), and the smallest by industry (15%).

This represents no change since 1950, when it was thought that this situation was only a temporary one, a reflection

Table 2. Institutions of Higher Learning in Israel, 1973. Total Student Enrollment and Academic Staff (also % in Natural Sciences)

Institution	Year founded	Student enrollment	Academic Staff Total	Natural sciences (% of total)
Technion	1924	8,608	1,328	1,328 (100%)
Hebrew University	1925	16,650	1,711	992 (58%)
Weizmann Institute (Sieff Inst.)	1949 (1934)	600	470	470 (100%)
Bar-Ilan University	1955	5,800	868	252 (29%)
Tel Aviv University	1962	11,700	2,036	672 (33%)
Haifa University	1963	3,600	527	0 (0%)
Ben-Gurion University of the Negev	1965	2,850	673	572 (85%)
TOTAL		49,800	7,610	4,286 (55%)

Central Bureau of Statistics

Table 3. Staff and Students in the Universities, by Faculty (1971/72)

	Humanities	Social Science	Law	Medicine
Staff	1,599	1,083	130	772
Students	15,346	10,211	2,225	1,875

Science & Mathematics	Agriculture	Engineering	Total *
2,179	100	871	6,734
6,793	9,049	8,077	45,676

* About 57% are in the natural sciences, medicine, agriculture, and engineering.

of the historical clinging to the ideology of knowledge for its own sake. Agricultural industry escaped this pitfall because it was linked to the "back to the land" ideology and was spurred on by the need for food. Medicine enjoyed a similar status resulting in a high life-expectancy (70.9 years for males, compared with 68.4 in Canada, 67.2 in Japan, and 66.6 in the United States). Though also very proud of its pure research, and even ready to extend grants

Table 4. Scientists in R & D according to Employment—1950, 1968, 1972

| | 1950 | | 1968 | | 1972 |
	USA	Israel	USA	Isreal	Israel
Industry	60%	17% (153)	71%	13% (370)	15% (1,000)
Government	20%	32% (337)	17%	27% (771)	20% (1,300)
Academic institutions	20%	51% (516)	12%	60% (1,700)	65% (4,286)
		1,006		2,841	6,586

far beyond its shores, the United States devotes only 5% of the Research and Development (R & D) budget to basic research, while 20% is given to applied research and 75% to engineering product development.

Expenditure on Research and Development. From Table 5 it can be seen that the State spent IL309 million in 1971/72. As in manpower, 63% of Government money was devoted to universities and only 7% to industry. Even these funds were probably devoted to machinery rather than manpower.

It is considered urgent and vital that Israel step up her application to industrial R & D so as to develop the industrial products necessary for economic independence, modern standards of living, security, and the creation of employment for graduate students and qualified immigrants who will in turn give impetus to the process. Aware of this, all those involved in the formulation of scientific and economic policy do everything to encourage the

Table 5. Current Expenditures for Civilian R & D in 1971 (IL million)

| User | Hospitals | Source of Finance | | | |
		Industry	Universities	Government	Total
Total	5	34	92	178	309
Government	0	1	0	53	54
Universities	0	1	92	111	204
Industry	0	32	0	13	45
Hospitals	5	0	0	1	6

development of science-based industries and creative applied research in industry.

The institutions of higher learning which constitute Israel's main technological and scientific strength have latterly begun to develop graduate schools in the applied sciences and science-based industries, concentrated in industrial parks in the area of the institutions. This is generating an active interest in canalizing the manpower of the academic institutions toward the solution of industrial problems and in mobilizing this source for applied science.

Despite all this encouragement, however, the practical economics and policies at present lead to private industry finding it impossible to set aside funds for research.

Whereas machinery is considered "safe" collateral for loans and investments, manpower and research are regarded with suspicion, and contracts are considered risky, since they might not fulfill expectations. The conditions vary from one enterprise to another, and from government to the private sector.

Patents. Another indicator of these policies is the adverse technological balance of payments (for technological knowledge, manufacturing licenses, and patents purchased against those which the country sells). In other words, Israel buys much more know-how than it creates. (Between 1960 and 1965 it sold know-how worth $1,000,000 and bought know-how for $8,000,000).

The application for registration of patents each year is one-fifth of those submitted in Holland and one-tenth of those in Sweden (Table 6): the majority are for trivial items. There has been little effort to convert active basic

Table 6. Number of Patents by Country of Origin, 1958–1963

U.S.	32	Switzerland	2.5	Denmark	0.5
Japan	19	Sweden	2.5	Norway	0.5
Germany	18	Holland	1.1	Finland	0.4
Great Britain	12	Belgium	0.8	Israel	0.2
France	7		Percentage of 2,000		

research into industrial processes, and many processes whose early phases were developed in the laboratories of research institutions in Israel were exploited by overseas buyers.

A change, however, has recently taken place. In Israel Mining Industries new processes have been developed for the exploitation of local mineral resources such as copper, phosphoric acid, phosphates, and magnesium. Government, Histadrut, and some private industries are developing petroleum products, plastics, and agricultural products. New methods of desalination are being developed, and the electronics, electrooptic, and aircraft industries are forging ahead.

There is thus a budding science-based industry in fields such as agriculture, chemistry, pharmaceuticals, electronics, engineering, and publishing, consisting of some 100 different enterprises.

Governmental Initiatives. Government bodies endeavor to rise to the challenge of rapid industrial development. Leading these is the National Council for Research and Development of the Prime Minister's Office, which advises the Government on science policy—research, planning, and technological development. It also initiates research considered of importance to the State, provides information, and organizes conferences. Since its foundation in 1949, it has aimed at the development of industry and agriculture, exploitation of the country's mineral resources, and the improvement of the health of the population. Members of the Council were leading scientists, and its work was carried out in several small committees of specialists. The Council proved to be an incubator for fledgling institutions such as the Geological Survey of Israel, the Dead Sea Research Laboratory, Israel Mining Industries, the National Physical Laboratory, the Israel Fiber Institute, the Weizmann Science Press, the Israel Program for Scientific Translations, the Negev Arid Zone Research Institute, and the National Center of Scientific and Technological Information. The majority of these were later transferred to various other ministries or to universities.

The Council also founded research associations which linked Government and industry. These were the Paint Association, the Rubber Research Association, and the Ceramic and Silicate Institute.

Within the Prime Minister's Office are also the Central Bureau of Statistics, the Israel Institute for Biological Research, and the Atomic Energy Commission with two nuclear research centers. The one at Naḥal Sorek has a 5-megawatt reactor and the other in the Negev a 25-megawatt reactor.

Other ministries with research departments are the Ministries of Agriculture (half the entire civilian Government research budget), Commerce and Industry, Development, Education and Culture, Finance, Health, Housing, Labor, Social Welfare, and Transport and Communications.

During the last few years, chief scientists have been appointed to the various ministries, whose work has been further coordinated through authorities in various fields which span the activities in the ministries, i.e., the Authorities for Agriculture and for Industry.

The Israel Academy of Sciences and Humanities. Founded in 1961 by a Law of the Knesset, the Academy consists of leading Israel scholars. It fosters and promotes work in the sciences and humanities, advises the Government on important national research and science activities, and maintains contact with similar bodies abroad.

Defense Research. Defense research has given an impetus to some of the applied research by contracting for projects and providing budgets for industry. In itself, it constitutes the largest research establishment in the country. It began during the War of Independence in the scientific branch of the army (*Hemed*), which worked in the scientific institutions, particularly the Weizmann Institute. Before long it had its own buildings and was transferred from the army to the Ministry of Defense. It includes at present the Research and Planning Department, the Authority for Weapon Development (Raphael), and Israel Military Industries.

International Relations. The scientific community of Israel enjoys high standing and is in close contact with colleagues abroad. The total number of scientists in Israel compares favorably with other countries both in quality and quantity (Table 7). There is a constant exchange between Israel's institutions and leading academic establishments abroad. An abundance of conferences take place at a high level, and the guest list is studded with eminent academicians and Nobel Prize laureates.

Table 7. Comparison of the Number of Scientists in Israel and Other Countries

Country	Scientists per 1,000 inhabitants	Country	Scientists per 1,000 inhabitants
U.S.	25	Belgium	6
Sweden	22	Holland	8
Canada	7	Italy	4
Germany	6	Japan	12
Great Britain	11	Israel	10.7
France	7		

3 INDUSTRIES USING ADVANCED TECHNOLOGY

There are in Israel about 100 firms with a labor force of 30,000, of whom 3,000 are engineers and scientists. About 1,000 of the engineers and scientists are engaged in R & D.

Israel Aircraft Industries. Founded by the Government in 1953 as Bedek Aviation, Israel Aircraft Industries is the only industry of sizable proportions, accounting for one-third of all Israel's technology-based industry. This is now a multi-faceted industrial complex employing 13,500 workers, 10% of whom are engineers and academic personnel.

One of the assembly sections of the Tadiran Semiconductor Plant.
Courtesy Tadiran, Tel Aviv.

Table 8. Percentage Shares of the World's Population, GNP (Wealth), and Scientific Publishing Manpower and Output

Country	Percentage population	Percentage GNP	Percentage scientists	Percentage papers on physics and chemistry	Percentage of patents*
U.S.	5.9	32.8	41.5	30.1	32.0
U.S.S.R.	7.0	15.6	8.0	18.2	—
Great Britain	1.6	4.8	8.1	10.2	12.0
France	1.4	4.5	5.4	5.4	7.0
Japan	2.9	3.6	4.1	7.6	19.0
Italy	1.5	2.6	2.2	3.1	—
Canada	0.6	2.2	3.2	1.6	—
India	14.4	2.2	2.3	2.0	—
Switzerland	0.2	0.6	1.4	1.0	2.5
Israel	0.08	0.12	0.9	0.6	0.2
South Africa	—	0.6	0.3		—
Austria	—	0.4	0.5	0.3	—
China	—	3.6	0.03		—

* Share of output of 200,000 patents between 1958 and 1963. Other percentages were: Germany, 18.0; Sweden, 2.5; Holland, 1.1.

Electronics. There are 44 firms employing 13,000 workers, of whom 10% are engineers and some mathematicians. Twenty-seven of the firms employ less than 100 workers each, seven between 100 and 400 workers, and five firms (Elron Electronic Industries, Motorola, Plant B—Israel Aircraft Industries, Elta, and Telrad Telecommunications and Electronic Industries) 1,000–1,500 workers each. Only one company, Tadiran Israel Electronics Industries, employs as many as 3,500 workers.

Chemicals, Pharmaceuticals, and Feed Additives. There are 21 firms employing 2,800 workers, of whom 380 are engineers or scientists. All of these have less than 300 workers each, except for one (Makhteshim Chemical Works, Beersheba) which employs 600.

Other Industries. There are eight small firms employing about 100 engineers and mathematicians for work in software and systems analysis. About 800 workers are employed in 12 firms in various fields such as water meter works, biomedical instruments, teaching aids, engines, plastics, and sterile packaging, editing, publishing, and translating.

Industrial Research Institutes. These are institutes established mainly by the National Council for Research and Development, but some also by the Technion, to assist industry by offering technical services, consultation, and dissemination of scientific and technological information and economic studies. About 500 persons are employed, of whom 25% are scientists. The largest of these institutes is Israel Mining Industries.

Institutions of Higher Learning. The academic institutions have established companies for the commercial exploitation of the results of their scientific research. They are also setting up industrial parks to provide central services and facilities for industries developing with their aid and encouragement. These companies and parks are: the Technion Research and Development Foundation, the Scientific Research Foundation (National Physical Laboratory), Yeda Research and Development (Weizmann In-

View of Makhteshim Beersheba, chemical works. Photo Mula and Haramaty, Tel Aviv.

stitute), Yissum Research Development Co. (Hebrew University), Atidim—Science-Based Industries (Tel Aviv University), Science-Based Industries Campus (Hebrew University), Sidco, Science-Based Industries Development Corp. (Weizmann Institute), and Sor-Van (Sorek Nuclear Research Center).

4 FIELDS OF SCIENCE

Exactly how the IL309 million (S71.2 million) allocated in 1972 was spent on various fields of scientific research is shown in Table 9 below. Scientists in civilian research worked on over 9,000 projects (compared to 3,000 in 1967). Most of these were in biology, medicine, and agriculture (47.4%), a decrease from 1967 (61.8%), since when engineering has increased from 4.5% to 12.7%, reflecting the effort to invest more in engineering research for the development of industry.

Another interesting trend is the diminishing role of chemistry, which in 1950 was proportionally Israel's major scientific field. Although it is still represented by a respectable 15.8%, this is a much lower figure than the 41.9% devoted to chemistry in 1950. Some factors contributing to

Table 9. Research in Israel according to Disciplines

Discipline	1950 %	1967 %	1972 %
Biology	13.5	21.2	16.2
Medicine	7.5	23.8	16.6
Agriculture	8.0	16.8	14.6
Chemistry & chemical engineering	41.8	13.5	15.8
Earth & space science	3.3 (earth)	6.0	6.3
Electronics & electrical engineering		1.5	4.1
Engineering (civil, mechanical, nuclear, aeronautics)	8.0		
		2.9	8.6
Materials science		1.2	2.6
Mathematics	4.2	1.1	5.5
Physics	13.7	11.2	9.6

M. Balaban and A. Katzir, NCRD Circular 9–73.

this decline are the inception and expansion of other fields and changing categorization of much basically chemical work under other fields such as biomedical research.

It is of interest to survey the various fields in which scientists in Israel are presently engaged. This is neither a comprehensive nor even a balanced summary of all fields mentioned in the table. Some will be dispersed under an interdisciplinary roof such as environment or natural resources, some subjects might be mentioned more than once in different contexts, smaller projects might be stressed because of their particular local significance, and others could have been omitted. However, it is hoped that the pulse and spectrum of scientific activity in Israel will still emerge.

Chemistry. Much of what is really chemical research is dispersed through other fields. The techniques and insights of chemistry are found in much of theoretical research, as it is a crucial factor in our daily life, contributing to the development, for example, of plastics, pharmaceuticals, and environmental well-being.

Israel is an important center for theoretical chemistry (molecular electronic quantum mechanics, etc.), and work in physical chemistry and chemical physics deals with subjects like radiation chemistry and the thermodynamics of polymers. Organic chemistry is well represented in the synthesis of natural products and in the development of efficient ways of synthesizing polyamino acids and peptides, which are produced for export. The polyamino acids, important in the study of man's biological makeup, provide an exciting field of research for biochemists. The study of polymers has made an important impact on subjects as diversified as plastics, desalination, and the conversion of chemical energy directly into mechanical energy. Chemistry's worldwide contribution to biology is reflected in Israel's laboratories. Enzymes, peptides, and other proteins are studied by magnetic resonance, while radioisotope research is carried out at the reactor centers (isotopes are widely used in medicine). Analytical and soil chemistry find their place among the wide range of subjects of concern to chemists: magnetic resonance using the oxygen-17 isotope is a specialty of Israel.

Other important chemistry-based industries produce pharmaceuticals, vitamins, ethical drugs, steroids, immunoglobins, cholera vaccine, plant growth regulators, and biodegradable detergents.

Israel's most extensive natural resource, the Dead Sea, inspired the first industrial research in the country — on potash and bromine—and phosphate deposits initiated the study of phosphorus chemistry. Industrial chemical research is now done at the universities, at Israel Mining Industries (IMI), and in the large chemical companies: Chemicals and Phosphates, Dead Sea Potash Co., Dead Sea Bromine Co., Negev Phosphates, and Makhteshim.

IMI is involved in process development and research on phosphoric acid, phosphate chemicals, fertilizer com-

The chemical plant at Arad, 1973. Courtesy Government Press Office, Tel Aviv.

pounds, petrochemicals, and polymers, minerals, plasma chemistry, materials, and ceramics. Chemicals and Phosphates works on fertilizers and fluoride; the Dead Sea Co. develops potash, magnesium chloride, and bromine; while Makhteshim is working on pesticides, fungicides, and organic compounds.

Biomedical Research. It is almost as impossible to draw a sharp line between applied and basic sciences as to delineate the border between clinical and theoretical research in the biomedical sciences. Biomedical research is carried out in the academic institutions and at hospitals, clinics, and various research institutes.

Israel has made significant contributions in the fields of cancer research, immunology, and research in cardiology and on blood vessels. About two-thirds of cancer research has been carried out at the Weizmann Institute on the pathology of the living cell.

MICROBIOLOGY. Reference laboratories are continually alert to detect, isolate, and diagnose dangerous organisms. Vaccines for man and livestock are being developed. Research is carried out to find new source materials for vaccine production or immunization such as attenuated strains, non-virulent mutations, or artificially enhanced immunogenicity of weak antigens. Some of the products of these methods are the basis of science-based industries.

Basic research carried out in the academic institutions includes biology of microbial and viral life forms; genetics, ecology, and population dynamics of bacteria; enzymes and biosynthetic pathways for nucleic acids and proteins; and microbiological membranes, the immune response, transplantation immunology, and antigenicity of substances.

Several types of cancer seem to originate from a DNA virus (leukemia and cancer of the breast). While virologists try to induce tumors with viruses, microbiologists endeavor to destroy the cancerous cell by using bacterial products to attack the changed membranes of the cancer cell, thus harnessing the immunological system of the body to seek out and destroy the abnormal cells.

MEDICAL RESEARCH. Important research has been undertaken in the study of the heart and blood vessels. Some other subjects are: the factors influencing immunity, the activity of hormones in reproduction, and the life cycle of disease-causing parasites. Impressive advances have been made in heart, brain, orthopaedic, and plastic surgery. In the field of bioengineering, instruments that have been developed include a new pacemaker, a tiny heart massager, a remote control instrument for recording the heart's activity, and an instrument for automatic control of artificial kidneys. Outstanding results have been achieved in community medicine and in the rehabilitation of war and accident victims.

An interesting specific study is being carried out on diseases and human genetics. Israel's varied population, with new immigrants from every part of the world, provides material for interesting genetic, ecological, and environmental-physiological observations. The first generations of different ethnic groups live side by side, preserving their different nutritional habits and cultures: the second generation quickly acquires the life patterns of modern Israel society. An especially interesting discovery was that Yemenites display a remarkably low frequency of circulatory and heart disease, apparently because of their special diet. Research has shown that changes in blood vessels begin in childhood, but find expression only later in life.

Apart from the Hebrew University—Hadassah Medical School, there is now a medical school at Tel Aviv University, while at Haifa and the Ben-Gurion University of the Negev other schools are being established.

AGRICULTURE. The economy of Israel is based primarily on agriculture, both for local consumption and for export. Agricultural research is carried out by the Faculty of Agriculture of the Hebrew University at Rehovot, the Agricultural Research Organization of the Ministry of Agriculture, and by the department of agricultural engineering of the Haifa Technion.

Since water is scarce, one of the first tasks of Israel agriculture was to make the most extensive use of the limited supplies (see Environment). Intensive research has led to a high irrigation efficiency with one of the highest yields in the world. Varieties thus chosen for their high yield potential are early groundnuts, paper-white narcissus, peppers resistant to virus diseases, early onions, and out-of-season melons. The dehydrating and deep freeze industries have stimulated research to produce vegetables suitable for mechanical harvesting.

While these vegetables are developed with the harvesting machinery in mind, the machines are being improved and adapted to suit the vegetables. Agricultural engineers are also improving farm structures, and introducing labor-saving methods and sprinkling equipment. To produce crops using little water, research is undertaken into crop rotation, fertilization, tillage, plant population, and weed control.

Research is carried out on both open-air and protected crops. To increase the production of such open-air crops as citrus, avocado, mango, lettuce, onions, artichokes, asparagus, iris, and gladioli, agricultural research workers endeavor to increase the yields, extend the harvesting season, and improve quality. Protected crops such as strawberries, carnations, chrysanthemums, and roses are grown under simple low plastic coverings, plastic tunnels, and unheated structures or in highly sophisticated greenhouses to provide the best conditions of light, ventilation, temperature, humidity, and soil.

Special emphasis has been laid on finding pest-control methods which do not cause pollution. Progress has been made in the biological control of insects in citrus, avocado, and date palm. The biology, ecology, and physiology of insect pests is under constant study.

ANIMAL HUSBANDRY. Dairy cattle usually never see a pasture and sheep are hand-fed. Milk production has been increased as a result of research which has shown that calves fertilized at the age of 8½ months instead of at 16 months produce 15% more milk. This, combined with highly intensive feeding methods, has resulted in one of the highest milk yields in the world.

VETERINARY RESEARCH. The Kimron Veterinary Institute investigates diseases in cattle, sheep, and birds. Some of the local diseases investigated are tick fever, foot-and-mouth disease, and staphylococcus infection of the udders of cattle.

Geology. The department of geology at the Hebrew University of Jerusalem, founded in 1927, dealt mainly with mapping the north and center of the country and with searching for underground water. Since the foundation of the State, other institutes which have sprung up are the Israel Geological Survey, the Geophysical and Oil Research Co., the Israel Institute of Petroleum, the Oceanographic and Limnological Research Co., the division of isotope chemistry at the Weizmann Institute, the department of mining engineering at the Technion, and most recently a department in the Ben-Gurion University of the Negev.

One of the most important activities has been the preparation and publishing of geological maps of the country, first on a 1:100,000, then 1:250,000, and more recently one on a 1:50,000 scale.

As a result of the geological mapping of the Negev, mineral prospecting was initiated by Israel Mining Industries Ltd. who are responsible for chemical R & D. The main deposits exploited are phosphates, salts of the Dead Sea, copper, and clays.

The Timna Copper Mines Co. now produces 12,000 tons of copper annually at the site of King Solomon's old quarry. Phosphates were found at Oron, Ef'eh, the Makhtesh ha-Katan, and elsewhere, and flint-clay deposits were discovered in Zefa in the Makhtesh Ramon. These raw

Students from Taiwan, Thailand, and India sampling dolomites near a fault zone west of Jericho, during a scientific trip of students from developing countries, March 1972. Courtesy Hebrew University Public Relations Department, Jerusalem. Photo David Harris, Jerusalem.

materials provide local supplies for the building industry, including cement, glass, ceramics, and refractory clays.

The search for oil led to the Ḥeleẓ oil fields and Zohar and Kanna'im gas fields. Petroleum prospecting uses seismic profiles and magnetometric and gravimetric surveys to discover potentially oil-laden underground structures. Intensive stepped-up research has been initiated recently in many parts of the country.

Whereas 25 years ago geology was a descriptive and qualitative science, today it is a genetic and quantitative exact science requiring sophisticated equipment.

A detailed study has been made on the stratigraphy and chronology of the rock sequence in Israel based on micro- and macro-paleontological and geochemical data.

Petrological study of magmatic, metamorphic, and sedimentary rocks today employs not only classical methods of the polarizing microscope and chemistry laboratory, but also X rays, atomic absorption spectroscopy, X ray fluorescence, optical spectroscopy, and the atomic accelerator. A study is being made of the most interesting Hatrurim metamorphic complex in the Judean Desert, where minerals were formed at very high temperatures by a metamorphic process previously unknown. Mineralogical research on the structure of clays has revealed their geographical and chronological distribution and established their environment of formation. The interrelationship between clay minerals and organo-metallic compounds has also been studied.

Research on rift valley formation is a natural subject for Israel, where the Syro-African rift valley, the largest in the world, lies along the Israel-Jordan border.

Oceanographic and limnological research has fascinating subjects in the Dead Sea, the Sea of Galilee, and the Red Sea for study of their natural history. Also of major interest are the East Mediterranean coast and continental shelf and the intermediate and deep zone of the southeastern Mediterranean. Wave motions, currents, sand transport, and the effect of man-made structures on the physical marine environment are being studied.

Micropaleontological research has begun, and geochemical studies have been undertaken, in order to examine chemical elements in nature and to further paleogeographical and paleo-ecological research, which is especially important in prospecting for mineral resources.

Scientists at the Weizmann Institute and the Hebrew University are also engaged in organic and isotope geochemistry of stable and radioactive elements, including rare gases. The Hebrew University has a geochronological laboratory to determine the absolute age of rocks and minerals.

OIL SCIENCE. R & D is concentrated at Oil Refineries

Ltd. in Haifa and at the Technion petroleum laboratory and the Standards Institution of Israel. The Israel Institute of Petroleum coordinates some of the research of oil companies, its technical department deals with projects such as underground storage, geological surveys, and studies on oil reserves, while the engineering staff deal with oil pollution of waterways, sea, and underground water.

Physics. The variety of fields in physics tackled in this small country includes elementary particles, quantum electronics, high energy, and nuclear, solid state, laser, and plasma physics. Recently Israel physicists have entered the fields of astronomy and astrophysics with the setting up by the Tel Aviv University of an observatory with a 40-inch telescope at Miẓpeh Ramon in the Negev.

There has been close collaboration between experimental and theoretical groups. The late Professor Giulio Racah of the Hebrew University, father of theoretical physics in Israel, influenced generations of students now working in the various other institutions. He established a school of atomic spectroscopy at the Hebrew University, and his students developed an important school of theoretical nuclear physics at the Weizmann Institute which made significant contributions to the development of the nuclear shell model. Later centers in the theory of elementary particles were developed at Tel Aviv University and the Weizmann Institute. Yuval Ne'eman made a very important contribution in 1961 when independently and concurrently with M. Gell-Mann, the Nobel Prize winner, he proposed the now famous SU_3 group symmetry as the basic symmetry for classifying fundamental particles of nature. An important contribution by high energy physicists has been one of the new central ideas in particle physics—"duality." A group at the Technion is associated with the renewed interest in general relativity and gravitation.

Solid state physics is an active field developing semiconductors, optical properties of crystals, magnetic materials, metals, superconductors, and crystal growth.

Since the discovery of the Moessbauer effect in 1957, this spectroscopy has been used for the study of hyperfine interactions in solids.

Quantum electronics includes development of new kinds of lasers and their application as a research tool in physics and other sciences.

Important geophysics studies have been undertaken at the Weizmann Institute on the propagation of seismic waves in the earth, and a seismic station has been set up near Eilat.

Lately more physicists have turned to applied fields connected with industrialization. Substantial work is being done in solar energy, the development of an electric car, and a reading machine for the blind at the National Physical Laboratory.

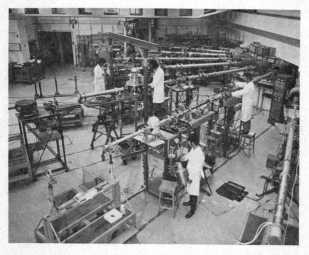

The target room of the Dannie N. Heinemann Accelerator Laboratory, Weizmann Institute of Science, where a check is being made of the beam tubes. Courtesy The Weizmann Institute of Science, Public Relations Office, Rehovot.

Model of the 19-story Koffler Accelerator Tower, the cornerstone for which was laid in 1973, at the Weizmann Institute of Science. The Tower will house a 14-UD Pelletron Accelerator (atom smasher). Courtesy The Weizmann Institute of Science, Public Relations Office, Reḥovot.

Experimental physics research often needs large and expensive equipment such as the new astronomical laboratory, a high voltage Van de Graaff Tandem Accelerator at Reḥovot, and a joint laboratory with the Hebrew University for studying nuclear reactions and basic nuclear properties.

NUCLEAR SCIENCE AND TECHNOLOGY. Basic research in nuclear physics comprises about 20% of physics research in Israel and is carried out at the five largest academic institutions (see above) and by the Atomic Energy Commission (AEC) which has two research reactors—the Naḥal Sorek Nuclear Research Center and the Negev Nuclear Research Center. At the reactors, and at the Technion, basic and applied research on reactor theory proceeds. The reactor centers actively cooperate with the Government and with industry. One way is to manufacture and improve radioisotopes and radiopharmaceuticals for biological research and medicine, and for original research, particularly resonance absorption and scattering induced by neutron captive gamma-rays.

A nuclear power plant of about 400 MW(e) is planned for the early 1980s and will perhaps be a dual-purpose power-desalination plant. In nuclear medicine there are about 12 hospitals employing radioisotope diagnostic procedures and operating radiotherapy units.

Industry widely applies industrial radiography using X ray and gamma-ray sources. The metal and machine industry has its own radiography service. A new company in the industrial park near the Sorek center, Sor-Van Radiation, offers sterilization services to manufacturers of medical disposables. Also based on AEC work are radiation-colored diamonds, and work is progressing on radiation in the plastics and textile industries.

Agriculture uses radiation to preserve fruits and vegetables (particularly onions and potatoes). Other projects include radiation-induced mutagenesis in plants, seed stimulation by low doses of radiation, and pest control by the sterile male release method.

Nuclear techniques are employed in the environmental and earth sciences. Radioactive tracers are used to study groundwater flow patterns, sewage dispersal in the sea, pollution dynamics in the National Water Carrier, neutron logging of water wells, and radiation processing of solid waste (see below, Environment).

The Elscint Ltd. company in Haifa produces and exports a broad and complete line of nuclear instruments for research, education, industry, and medicine. Seforad Ltd. in the Jordan Valley specializes in highly sophisticated detection equipment. Other items manufactured are smoke and fire detectors and soil moisture monitors.

Mathematics. Research in pure and applied mathematics, including statistics and computer science, is carried out mainly at the academic institutions. Local and

Working on a computer-controlled wiring instrument, Haifa, 1973.
Courtesy Government Press Office, Tel Aviv.

foreign scientists contribute to two major publications,
the *Journal d'Analyse Mathématique*, devoted to analysis, and the monthly *Israel Journal of Mathematics*, which
includes articles on all branches of pure mathematics. A
further indication of the worldwide nature of Israel research are international symposia such as the one on Partial Differential Equations and the Geometry of Normed
Linear Spaces held in Jerusalem in June 1972.

Engineering. Engineering research is carried out mainly
at the Technion, Israel's oldest technological institution,
whose functions grew together with the practical needs of
the State. Thus, to cope with the first need—water—hy-
draulic and civil engineers and geologists were trained.
Chemical engineering soon followed, in order to help
develop natural resources and food technology. The following activities are largely conducted by engineers trained
at the Technion.

AERONAUTICAL ENGINEERING. When an aeronautical

engineering department was founded at the Technion in 1951, it was looked at askance since all that Israel had was a glider club and refueling facilities at an international airport. It was from these beginnings, however, that the aircraft industry, now as large as all other industries in Israel combined, finally emerged. Based mainly on technologically trained manpower, the designing and construction of aircraft has become a worthwhile industry with a high added value. The raw material costs 30¢ a pound and the product sells for $200. In comparison, raw materials for cars cost 15¢ a pound and the finished product only $1. The "Arava" plane is the first product of this effort.

ELECTRONICS AND ELECTRICAL ENGINEERING. More than a quarter of the Technion's students graduate in these subjects. This reflects the rapid development of the industry, which has grown from IL100 million in 1965 to IL1,000 million in 1972. Though still small by international standards, manpower is the basis for its further growth.

Applied research deals with solid state devices and integrated circuits, digital and hybrid techniques, and computer applications. There are laboratories for microelectronics, electronic instrumentation, and electrooptics.

The medical electronics and bioengineering laboratories cooperate with hospitals in basic research into the biological control systems. Electronic instruments for this research particularly emphasize cardiovascular, neuromuscular, and control nervous systems.

In the electrical machinery and drives laboratory, new trends in power electronics and application of semiconductors to speed control of electrical machinery are being investigated.

The Weizmann Institute has a department of electronics involved mainly in magnetism, modern optics and biomedical engineering. New methods of efficient output coupling in various high power lasers are studied. The department of applied mathematics continues its highly intricate Golem B computer project.

Environment. As in the rest of the world, Israel has 137 also begun to take steps for the control of environmental ills such as air, water, and soil pollution and is hopeful of nipping some encroaching contaminants in the bud.

Work has been carried out for some time now on the physiology of man under extreme climatic conditions and on housing design, in order to help the population adapt to the desert climate prevailing in a large part of the country.

WATER. Israel is faced with the problem of an ever-increasing demand for water on the one hand, and depletion and pollution of supplies on the other.

Geologists continue the search for water using their knowledge of structural formation, and chemists have developed an isotope method using the rare H_2O isotope tritium as a tracer to track down underground water.

Chemists and engineers are seeking improved methods for the treatment and disposal of solid wastes so that these will not contaminate water supplies. Some of this work is a spin-off of the reverse osmosis method of desalination research. The same membranes developed for the desalination of water are useful for the removal of various troublesome wastes. Laboratories recently established by the Oceanographic & Limnological Co. have been studying the purification and reutilization of sewage. Mekorot, the National Water Carrier, and Tahal—Water Planning for Israel have long been active in water quality research. Sewage purification projects were underway in the 1950s, recycling water for reuse in homes, industry, and agriculture, and there is a project of this kind for the Tel Aviv metropolitan area, where water is run back into the system for use after remaining three years underground.

There are, however, other ways to utilize precious water. One is the use of brackish water for certain crops: botanists and agricultural research workers have tried to determine which plants could grow in brackish water, making it possible to utilize such water in the Negev. They are also growing plants in areas with a very small rainfall, making use of dew and runoff.

Israel has one of the world's highest efficiencies in the use of water for irrigation. The radically new system of trickle irrigation—applying water slowly and continuously from drippers regularly spaced along the plant rows and permanent installations of low-intensity sprinklers—has produced dramatic results revolutionizing the whole concept of efficient irrigation. Apart from the use of less water, this method produces higher yields as the roots are kept constantly at nearly-optimal moisture, preventing excessive wetting or drying of the soil.

An active desalination program which is geared to solve the encroaching water shortage during the next decade is described below.

AIR. Air pollution occurs mainly along the highly populated coastal plain. Israel's sunny climate enhances smog through photochemical reactions. Scientists are studying the effects of air pollution on plants and human health. In the procedure for removing these pollutants they are first identified, the climate affecting their formation and dispersion studied, and then legal and technological steps are taken to prevent or reduce atmospheric pollution.

NOISE. Noise pollution resulting from extensive building and industrialization is intensified by the fine climate in Israel which enables windows to be kept open throughout most of the year.

SOIL. Intensive agriculture relies on the use of great quantities of chemicals, including pesticides and fertilizers. Some of these persist and accumulate and may harm desirable species as well as pests, or find their way into lakes or percolate into groundwater and pollute wells. Greater awareness of the dangers of pollution has recently stimulated research to prevent it.

ADAPTING TO ARID AREAS. In several desert areas rainfall is sufficient for plant growth, but much of the water is lost and even causes denudation and erosion. Studies of revegetation and plant introduction show promising results.

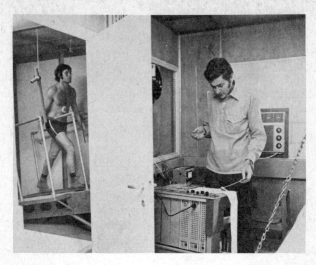

Test investigating man's physical capabilities under heat stress as part of research on man's adaption to heat. Courtesy Ben-Gurion University of the Negev, Beersheba. Photo David Harris, Jerusalem.

Studies on human health and work efficiency in a hot environment have made it possible to avoid conditions incompatible with work.

ORGANIZATION. A number of bodies were established between 1970 and 1973 to deal with the improvement of environmental quality. These are the Environmental Protection Service (of the Prime Minister's Office and National Council for Research and Development, to advise the Government), the Committee on the Biosphere and Environmental Quality of the NCRD, and the Israel Academy of Sciences, which is responsible for research.

Desalination. In 1972, Israel consumed 1,540 million cubic meters (mcm) of water, which means that 70 mcm had to be taken from one-time reserves. If drawing from these reserves continues, it is estimated that they will be ex-

Equipment for desalination experiments in a pilot plant at the Ben-Gurion University of the Negev. Courtesy Ben-Gurion University of the Negev, Beersheba. Photo David Harris, Jerusalem.

hausted by the end of the century. Desalination research is thus a vital need, and the Water Desalination Bureau of the NCRD, responsible for overall planning, analysis, and funding of R&D was set up in 1970. IL8-9000,000 are spent annually by 100 scientists and engineers who are moving desalination from the laboratory to the pilot stage, demonstration plant, and prototype phases.

VAPOR COMPRESSION PROCESS. Alexander Zarchin pioneered the development of the vacuum freezing-vapor compression process in Israel. Israel Desalination Engineering (IDE), a Government company, was founded on the basis of this process in 1966. Although the process itself has been abandoned, the compressor developed was transplanted to the successful ambient temperature vapor compression plant. Limited by the size of the compressor, the possible maximum size of such plants is 600 cubic meters of water per day. A special feature of these plants is their ability to use low-cost aluminum tubing instead of copper alloy. IDE's first commercial plant was marketed in 1966.

MULTI-EFFECT DISTILLATION PROCESS. To exploit Israel's integrated water supply grid and build large centralized desalination plants, IDE developed the multiple-effect distillation process which is free from the size limitation of the VC plants since there is no compressor. The process operates at lower temperatures and pressures than other distillation processes and cost calculations show that it should be 20–35% lower than in a multistage flash plant. This process is the basis of a joint U.S.–Israel project agreed upon in November 1972, designated for incorporation into the larger plants to be constructed from 1985 onward. A pilot plant was built in 1970, and the first large-scale demonstration plant producing 3,800 cubic meters per day (1 million gallons p.d.) was opened in 1973. This will be followed by the construction of a 40,000 cu m/day (11 mgd) prototype expected to begin operation in 1978.

MULTISTAGE FLASH DISTILLATION (MSF). Decided upon in 1962, an MSF plant began supplying Eilat with 3,800 cu m/day (1 mgd) in 1965, and in 1969 a similar plant was added to supply Eilat's growing population with almost 7,600 cu m/day (2 mgd) of water. The product is blended with brackish water pumped to Eilat from the Yotvatah area to produce an acceptable quality of water. Research has improved corrosion and scale prevention.

THE KOGAN-ROSE PROCESS. Profesor A. Kogan of the Technion's aeronautical engineering department, with the support of an industrialist named Rose, has developed an original MSF process with direct contact condensation of the vapors on a stream of cooler distillate. A pilot plant has been operating since 1970. It is hoped that this original method will provide dramatic savings by eliminating the expensive miles of piping needed in other processes.

CLOUD SEEDING PROGRAMS. Stimulating "artificial rain" by cloud seeding, which has been in progress for a decade, indicates that rain can be increased by 15% in northern and central Israel, providing up to some 150,000,000 cu m annually (410,000 cu m/day = 100 mgd).

ELECTRODIALYSIS. Electrodialysis research, begun in 1958 at the Negev Institute for Arid Zone Research in Beersheba to desalt brackish water, resulted in the use of well water by a 500 cu m/day demonstration plant in operation at Ze'elim since 1965. Membranes of various local and foreign makes have been tested and electrodes, gaskets, and scale prevention processes have been developed and evaluated.

The Ze'elim plant served as a pilot scheme for a partially UN-funded plant ordered in 1967 for Mashabbei Sadeh. The first plant, producing 2,400 cu m/day (almost 2/3 mgd), began operation in 1971 and it is planned to double its capacity.

REVERSE OSMOSIS. In 1968, the first plant of 200 cu m/day (1/19 mgd) capacity was built at Yotvatah, about 40 km north of Eilat, based on work at the Negev Institute begun in 1967. A number of locally developed plants now operate in various parts of the country, and various plants are being evaluated by the Mekorot Water Company at a test station in Eilat.

Outstanding theoretical and technological research on membranes for this process is actively pursued at the Weizmann Institute and the Negev Institute. Apart from their importance for desalination, membranes are also used in water softening and in sewage and waste water treatment.

SEWAGE AND WASTE WATER TREATMENT. About 140,000,000 cu m of reclaimed sewage water could be reused every year. At present, only 34,000,000 cu m are utilized, but quality and health standards must still be improved. Contaminants to be removed are bacteria, viruses, organic and inorganic chemicals, and salt. Various membrane separation processes are used to deal with two categories of sewage: industrial wastes, and municipal sewage. Industry aims to remove contaminants at source in order to prevent the poisoning of municipal sewage by heavy chemicals and to purify the plants' waste so as to allow in-plant water recycling, thus reducing its fresh water needs.

Many different concepts are being studied in different laboratories. As work moves into the field requiring greater financial outlay, a selection of these concepts will be utilized, after evaluation of the results, in long-range policy planning.

In 1971, groups working on the desalination of brackish water were expanded to include sewage reclamation.

The high degree of purification made possible by membrane separation processes might make the complete recycling of urban and industrial water supplies feasible, and a number of promising approaches are now being explored.

GLOSSARY

Aggadah, name given to those sections of Talmud and Midrash containing homiletic expositions of the Bible, stories, legends, folklore, anecdotes, or maxims.

Agudat Israel (Agudah), world organization of ultra-Orthodox Jews.

Aliyah, (1) immigration to Erez Israel; (2) one of the waves of immigration dating from the 1880s (First Aliyah, Second Aliyah, etc.).

Diaspora, Jews living in the "dispersion" outside Erez Israel; area of Jewish settlement outside Erez Israel.

Erez Israel, Land of Israel; Palestine.

Gadna, Israel government youth movement for training 13- to 18-year-olds in defense and national service.

Hadassah, Women's Zionist Organization of America.

Ḥeder (pl. **ḥadarim,** lit. "room"), school for teaching children Jewish religious observance.

Hilfsverein (abbr. for Hilfsverein der Deutschen Juden), the central charitable association of German Jewry, active 1901–41.

Histadrut (abbr. for Heb. Ha-Histadrut ha-Kelalit shel ha-Ovedim ha-Ivriyyim be-Erez Yisra'el), Erez Israel Jewish Labor Federation, founded in 1920; subsequently renamed Histadrut ha-Ovedim be-Erez Yisra'el.

Ḥovevei Zion, early (pre-Herzlian) Zionist movement in Russia.

Jewish Agency, the Zionist Organization's administrative body in Erez Israel until 1948; thereafter, a non-governmental body concerned with immigration, agricultural settlement, education, youth affairs, economic development, etc., acting on behalf of the World Zionist Organization.

Kibbutz (pl. **kibbutzim**), large communal settlement in Erez Israel based mainly on agriculture, but also engaging in industry.

145

Knesset, parliament of the State of Israel.

Mizrachi, world movement of religious Zionists.

Moshav (pl. **moshavim**), smallholders' cooperative agricultural settlement in Erez Israel.

Naḥal, pioneer youth branch of the Israel Defense Forces training cadres for agricultural settlement.

Negev, the southern, mostly arid, region of Israel.

ORT, world organization for the development of skilled trades and agriculture among the Jews.

R & D, research and development.

Seker, annual scholastic test to determine suitability for post-primary academic education.

Talmud, compendium of rabbinic legal teaching and discussion.

Talmud torah, term generally applied to Jewish religious (and ultimately to talmudic) study; also to traditional Jewish religious public schools.

Ulpan (pl. **ulpanim**), intensive Hebrew-language course for adults.

Va'ad Le'ummi, national council of the Jewish community in Erez Israel during the period of the British Mandate.

WIZO, Women's International Zionist Organization, active outside the U.S. and Canada (where its counterpart is Hadassah).

Yeshivah (pl. **yeshivot**), Jewish traditional academy devoted primarily to study of rabbinic literature.

Yishuv, settlement; more specifically, the Jewish community of Erez Israel in the pre-State period.

Youth Aliyah, organization founded in the early 1930s for the purpose of rescuing Jewish children and young persons from the Nazis, transferring them to Erez Israel and educating them there. With the support of the Jewish Agency, its work has since been greatly extended.

BIBLIOGRAPHY

Education

Hebrew University, *Calendar* (1925–).

idem., *Scopus—A Periodical Magazine* (1946–).

idem., *Report by the President* (1953–).

idem, *Research Reports* (1965–).

E. Rieger, *Ha-Ḥinnukh ha-Ivri be-Ereẓ Yisra'el*, 2 vols. (1940).

Haifa Technion, *Technion Bulletin*, 1–8 (1941–48), superseded by: *Technion, Israel Institute of Technology*, 1–17 (1949–66).

idem., *Technion Yearbook*, 1–23 (1942–66).

idem., *Toledot ha-Technion be-Reshito* (1953).

idem., *The President's Report and Reports of Other Officials* (1954–).

idem., *Technion Catalogue* (1955–66).

idem., *Technion: A Bi-Monthly of Features, News and Events* (1965–).

Histadrut ha-Morim, *Sefer ha-Yovel 1903-1943* (1946).

L. Levenson, *Vision and Fulfillment* (1950).

M. Avidor, *Education in Israel* (1957).

Weizmann Institute of Science, *Reḥovot* (Eng., 1959–).

R. Calder, *The Hand of Life: The Story of the Weizmann Institute* (1959).

Enẓiklopedyah Ḥinnukhit, 5 vols. (1961–68).

N. Bentwich, *The Hebrew University of Jerusalem 1918-1960* (1961).

M. Rutenberg, *Tenu'ot No'ar be-Yisra'el u-va-Olam* (1962), includes bibliography.

B. Shaḥar, *Workers' Education in Israel* (1962).

idem., *Tarbut ve-Ḥinnukh ba-Histadrut* (1965).

Be-Ḥinnukh u-ve-Tarbut, 28 (1962), 25–29; 31–32 (1964), 3–47.

H. Barzel, *Tenu'at ha-No'ar, Koroteha ba-Ammim u-ve-Yisra'el* (1963).

N. Levin, *Ma'avak ha-Rishonim al Yi'ud ha-Technion* (1964).

J. S. Bentwich, *Education in Israel* (1965), includes bibliography.

Israel Ministry of Education and Culture, *School Comes to Adults* (1965).

idem., *Hishtallemut Mevuggarim* (1965).

idem., *Advanced Adult Education in Israel* (1967).

UNESCO, *World Survey of Education*, Vol. IV, "Higher Education" (Paris, 1966).

idem., *Statistical Yearbook* (1967).

C. Weizmann, *Trial and Error* (1966), see index.

A. Ben-Yosef, in: *Sefer ha-Shanah shel Bar-Ilan*, 4–5 (1967), 12–29.

J. Wechsberg, *A Walk through the Garden of Science: A Profile of the Weizmann Institute* (1967).

A. F. Kleinberger, *Society, Schools and Progress in Israel* (1969).

H. Parzen, in: *Jewish Social Studies* (July 1970), 187–213.

L. Shultz (ed.), *Gateway to Science: The Weizmann Institute at Twenty-Five* (1970).

Israel Government Year Book.

Israel Central Bureau of Statistics, *Statistical Abstract 1973*, 620–650.

Science

P. Abelson, *Science*, 180 (4083) (1973), 259.

S. Adler in: *Mada*, 13 (1968), 78–79.

E.D. Bergmann, et. al., *Scripta Academica Hierosolymitana*, (1938–39).

M. Buber, et. al., *Eine Juedische Hochschule*, (1902).

D.J. De Solla Price, in: *Proceedings of the Israel Academy of Science and Humanities*, 4 (6) (1970).

Y. Dudai, *Scientific Research in Israel* (1974).

U. Hurwitz and M. Yavne, in: E. Tal and Y. Ezrachi (eds.), *Science Policy and Development* (1972).

E. Katchalski, *Doḥ ha-Va'adah li-Vedikat Irgun ha-Meḥkar ha-Memshalti ve-Nihulo* (Dec. 1968).

A. Katchalsky and M. Balaban, in: *Rivon le-Kalkalah*, (2 (7) (1955), 218–228.

S. Katz, in: *Mada, 213 (1968), 82–87.*

C. Keren and P. Wollman, *Current Research and Development Projects in Israel, Natural Sciences and Technology* (1972).

INDEX

152